CHRISTMAS ENTERTAINING

Also by BARBARA MYERS

CHRISTMAS COOKIES & CANDIES
GREAT DINNER PARTIES
WOMAN'S DAY OLD-FASHIONED DESSERTS

CHRISTMAS ENTERTAINING

Barbara Myers

Rawson, Wade Publishers Inc.
New York

Library of Congress Cataloging in Publication Data

Myers, Barbara.
   Christmas entertaining.

   Includes index.
   1. Christmas cookery.   2. Entertaining.   I. Title.
TX739.M93   1980   641.5'68   80-51252
ISBN 0-89256-144-0

Published simultaneously in Canada by
McClelland and Stewart, Ltd.
Manufactured in the United States of America by
GL—to come
Designed by Joan Croom
First Edition

American Book–Stratford Press, Inc.
Saddle Brook, New Jersey

Dedicated to John Dana Kushan

CONTENTS

CHRISTMAS ENTERTAINING

INTRODUCTION

The holiday period that surrounds Christmas and the New Year is the time for entertaining, and for most of us the favorite time of year to be a guest, a host, or a hostess. The festive decorations, the giving of gifts, and the heightened expectations of the season are all made for sharing.

Christmas Entertaining is a comprehensive source book for the variety of entertaining these holidays make possible: for morning get-togethers, an afternoon open house, evening cocktail parties, large buffet dinners, and casual unexpected visitors. For each situation special foods are necessary, and each recipe in this book was selected because it leads to something special.

The book is arranged by kinds of food and drink rather than by types of entertaining, so that you may choose from all categories in designing your own special holiday hospitality. This book provides the parts; you put the parts together.

The first section, "Holiday Punches and Drinks," includes eggnogs, hot drinks, punches—with or without alcohol—and some favorite standard cocktails that can be made in quantity. Whether you do your holiday entertaining in St. Paul or St. Petersburg, there is a recipe here for your wassail bowl.

"Christmas Breads" is a representation of holiday recipes gathered from both European and American sources. The European recipes are represented by butter-rich yeast breads, filled with fruits and nuts, specially shaped, and attractively decorated—the types of breads one associates with the Old World. The American counterpart is the tea bread (or loaf bread), which is sweeter and has a close resemblance to cake.

Next is a section of cold canapés, dips, and spreads, followed by one that features hot hors d'oeuvres. Though they are usually associated with stand-up cocktail parties, these foods fit well into any gathering where fingers, toothpicks, and spreading knives are the main utensils. So savory and full-flavored are these appetizers, a selection from the two categories could substitute for a meal. All are so delicious, your guests will know that a special occasion is in progress.

When more substantial fare is called for, turn to the section on cold buffet dishes. Here are the holiday mainstays—turkey, chicken, beef, and ham—prepared in varieties of ways that will delight the taste, create the holiday feeling at the buffet, and keep the hosts free to enjoy the party. In addition, there is a complement of side dishes—salads, marinated vegetables, and relishes—which will attractively fill out the buffet table.

The final section, "Holiday Sweets," is perhaps the most versatile of all. Many of the recipes included here belong at holiday socials, regardless of time of day or the size of party. There is a representation of European specialties, American interpretations, and old-fashioned simplicity. You will find in this section, cakes, tortes, pastries, and fruit specialties—as well as small delights which can be eaten out of hand.

The recipes for each of the categories in *Christmas Entertaining* were selected, not only for their appropriateness for the Christmas season, but also because they are ones which can be prepared in advance. Some dishes are easy to produce; others are relatively difficult; some are simple in

4

their presentation, yet others are festive in their decor. And all are delicious.

Whatever the occasion, you are certain to find in this collection of year-end traditional food, and special delicacies, numerous dishes which will fulfill your own interpretation of Christmas entertaining.

ḤOLIDAY PUNCḤES AND DRINKS

Assembled here is an array of punches such as traditional, rich and creamy Pendennis Club Eggnog; Christmas Wassail, a warming brew of fragrant and spicy cider laced with rum; and Tom and Jerry, another hot cup made from a spicy batter. Among the lighter punches are Strawberry Bowl, sparkling with champagne; White Sangria made with Chablis and a garnish of fruits; and Cranberry Punch, a non-alcoholic fruit punch. And there are cocktails, which may be made in quantity, such as President Madison's Whiskey Sours; and One-Two-Three Daiquiris, served icy cold from the freezer.

OLD-FASHIONED EGGNOG

A standard part of American Christmas tradition. For a festive presentation, serve the eggnog from a silver or crystal punch bowl, surrounded with fresh holly.

12 eggs, separated

¾ cup sugar

2 cups bourbon whiskey

1 quart milk

1 quart heavy cream

2 cups cognac

Nutmeg, freshly grated

Beat the egg yolks in an electric mixer until they are light and lemon in color. Slowly add the sugar; continue beating until thick and creamy, and the sugar has completely dissolved.

Add the bourbon slowly (to prevent curdling), while beating at low speed. Stir in the milk and cream, then the cognac. Chill overnight.

Just before serving, beat the egg whites until they are stiff enough to stand in firm peaks and fold into the egg yolk mixture. Blend lightly but thoroughly.

Serve in a punch bowl, sprinkling the top lightly with nutmeg.

Makes about 4 quarts, or 32 punch-cup servings.

PENDENNIS CLUB EGGNOG

This famous eggnog originated in the Pendennis Club in Louisville, Kentucky. Egg yolks are used instead of whole eggs, and whipped cream is substituted for milk. The result is surely the richest of all versions; it is also the thickest and should be consumed by the spoonful.

3 **cups bourbon whiskey**

1½ **cups sugar**

9 **egg yolks**

6 **cups heavy cream (3 pints)**

Nutmeg, freshly grated

Combine the bourbon and sugar in a mixing bowl; let stand at least 3 hours to dissolve the sugar. Stir well.

Beat the egg yolks until slightly thickened and pale yellow in color. Gradually stir them into the bourbon mixture. Blend well. Let stand 2½ to 3 hours. (This will *cook* the egg yolks, taking away the raw flavor.)

Beat the cream until stiff; fold into the bourbon mixture. Refrigerate until thoroughly chilled (at least 1 hour); then turn into a punch bowl and sprinkle the top lightly with nutmeg. Serve in punch cups.

Makes about 30 punch-cup servings.

Note: This punch is actually more suitable to serve as dessert. To make it drinkable, thin to the desired consistency by diluting with cold milk. Whip the milk in with a wire whisk just before serving.

ORANGE EGGNOG FLOAT

A nonalcoholic fruit juice and ginger ale punch with islands of vanilla ice cream floating on top.

4 eggs

6 tablespoons sugar

5½ cups fresh orange juice, chilled

½ cup lemon juice

1 quart vanilla ice cream

1 quart ginger ale, chilled

Beat the eggs with the sugar until light. Stir in the orange juice and lemon juice.

Place small scoops of the ice cream in a punch bowl. Pour in the ginger ale against the sides of the bowl.

Add the orange juice mixture slowly, stirring gently. Serve immediately.

Makes about 4 quarts, or 30 punch-cup servings.

COFFEE ROYALE

A sweet, creamy punch ideal for midafternoon.

- 1 jar (2 ounces) instant coffee
- 2 cups sugar
- 2 cups boiling water
- 2 quarts light cream
- 1 quart sparkling water, chilled
- 1 cup brandy
- 2 cups heavy cream, whipped
- Block of ice or ice ring

Add the coffee granules and sugar to the boiling water; stir until both are dissolved. Cool, then refrigerate until ready to serve.

Place a block of ice in a punch bowl. Pour the coffee syrup, light cream, sparkling water, and brandy over the ice.

Spoon the whipped cream over the top; stir lightly to blend.

Makes 4½ quarts, or 36 punch-cup servings.

SEAFOAM PUNCH

Pale, with a foamy green cap. Easy and exceptional.

1 quart lime sherbet

2 quarts ginger ale, chilled

Mash the sherbet with a large spoon, or use an electric mixer. Turn the sherbet into a punch bowl.

Add the ginger ale; stir until the sherbet melts slightly.
Makes 3 quarts, or 24 punch-cup servings.

MILK PUNCH

The secret here is to serve the mixture icy cold.

1½ cups bourbon or rye whiskey

¼ cup superfine sugar

6 cups milk

Nutmeg, freshly grated

Pour the bourbon or rye into a pitcher. Add the sugar and stir until dissolved. Stir in the milk. (This punch may be served immediately, but the flavor is improved if it is refrigerated for several hours.)

When ready to serve, add several ice cubes, stir vigorously until the mixture is icy cold, then strain into old-fashioned glasses. Sprinkle with nutmeg.

Makes 15 4-ounce servings.

TOM AND JERRY

A traditional American holiday drink made from a spicy batter. Served very hot, it is the perfect cup for welcoming friends from the cold outdoors.

6 eggs

1 teaspoon vanilla extract

1 teaspoon nutmeg, freshly grated

1 teaspoon ground cinnamon

½ teaspoon ground cloves

½ teaspoon ground allspice

¼ teaspoon ground ginger

1 pound confectioners' sugar (about)

Rum or brandy (or both)

Near-boiling water

Separate the eggs. Using an electric mixer, beat the yolks with the vanilla, nutmeg, cinnamon, cloves, allspice, and ginger until light. Gradually beat in the confectioners' sugar, adding enough to make a very stiff batter. (Beat in as much sugar as you can; the amount will depend on the size of the egg yolks.)

Beat the egg whites until they are stiff, but not dry. Stir a heaping tablespoon of the egg whites into the egg yolk batter, then fold in the remainder. (May be made to this point and refrigerated; it will hold for at least 4 hours.)

For each serving, add a heaping tablespoon of the batter to a small mug (4 to 6 ounces) or coffee cup. Add a jigger

14

(1½ ounces) of rum or brandy (or 1 ounce rum and ½ ounce brandy). Fill the mug with near-boiling water and stir until frothy.

Makes enough for 24 servings.

CHRISTMAS WASSAIL

Wassail—a toast to your health. This punch is a warming brew of fragrant and spicy cider laced with rum. It is served from a bowl attractively garnished with decorated orange slices.

- 1 **gallon apple cider**
- 4 **juice oranges**
- 2 **lemons**
- 1 **tablespoon whole cloves**
- 1 **tablespoon whole allspice**
- 4 **cinnamon sticks, broken**
  - **Sugar, to taste**
- 1 **quart dark rum**

Pour the apple cider into a large saucepan or kettle.

Strip the peels from the oranges and lemons, using a vegetable peeler. (Trim only the zest, none of the white.) Add the peels to the cider. Squeeze the juice from the oranges and lemons; add. Stir in the cloves, allspice, and cinnamon sticks.

Bring the mixture to a boil, then reduce the heat and simmer 15 minutes. Taste, then add sugar to sweeten as necessary. Allow to cool, then strain to remove the rinds and spices. Set aside in a cool place until ready to serve; it is not necessary to refrigerate.

To serve, reheat the spiced cider with the rum; do not allow it to boil. Pour into a heat-proof punch bowl. Ladle into small mugs or punch cups.

Makes about 5 quarts, or 40 punch-cup servings.

Note: For an attractive garnish, insert 4 whole cloves into the rims of 4 thick orange slices, and spear each slice with a short piece of cinnamon stick in the center. Float in the wassail bowl when serving.

HOT MULLED WINE

This wine punch may be prepared days in advance. It is the perfect hot drink to serve after a cold winter outing.

1 **cup sugar**

2 **cups water**

Juice of 1 lemon (2 tablespoons)

1 **tablespoon whole cloves**

1 **tablespoon whole allspice**

6 **cinnamon sticks**

2 **quarts Burgundy wine**

Combine the sugar, water, lemon juice, and spices in a large saucepan. Stir over medium heat until the sugar dissolves; then cover and simmer 20 minutes.

Add the wine; heat just until bubbles appear around the edge; do not boil. Strain.

Serve hot in small mugs or punch cups.

Makes about 20 4-ounce servings.

Note: If the punch is made in advance, strain out the spices before storing.

17

A CHRISTMAS PUNCH

A lightly minted punch with a pineapple juice base—tasty served alone or with vodka. To chill the punch, add an ice ring frozen with red carnations or holly leaves with red berries.

4 cans (46 ounces each) unsweetened pineapple juice, chilled

½ cup green crème de menthe

2 cups vodka (optional)

Decorative ice ring (method follows)

Combine the pineapple juice, crème de menthe, and vodka in a punch bowl. Float the ice ring on top. Ladle into punch cups for serving.

Makes about 6 quarts, or 50 punch-cup servings.

DECORATIVE ICE RING

Fill a ring mold with distilled water (for the clearest ice) or tap water. (Leave space in the mold for garnish and expansion.) If tap water is used, let stand several hours to eliminate the air bubbles. Float a few red carnations or holly leaves with berries on the surface, then freeze. Dip the mold in warm water to remove the ice ring.

CRANBERRY PUNCH

Nonalcoholic and nice.

   2 cans (12 ounces each) frozen orange juice
      concentrate, thawed
   6 cups cranberry juice
   4 quarts ginger ale, chilled
      Block of ice or ice ring

Combine the orange juice (not diluted) and cranberry juice; chill. When ready to serve, pour over a block of ice in a punch bowl. Add the ginger ale, carefully pouring it down the side of the bowl; mix lightly.

Makes about 6 quarts, or 48 punch-cup servings.

   Note: For a simple garnish, strip the peel vertically from an orange with a lemon zester at quarter-inch intervals. Cut the notched oranges across in thin slices; float on top of the punch, along with a few fresh cranberries, if desired.

SPARKLING FRUIT PUNCH

Colorful; made without spirits.

  1 **cup sugar**
  ½ **cup water**
  2 **cans (6 ounces each) frozen limeade concentrate,**
     thawed
  1 **package (10 ounces) frozen strawberries,**
     chopped while frozen
  1 **quart ice water**
  2 **bottles (28 ounces each) sparkling water, chilled**
  1 **lime, thinly sliced**

Combine the sugar and the ½ cup water in a saucepan. Cook and stir until the sugar is dissolved; boil 3 minutes. Cool.

Combine the sugar syrup, limeade (not diluted), strawberries, and the ice water in a punch bowl. Add ice. Pour in the sparkling water and float the lime slices on top.
Makes 3½ quarts, or about 30 punch-cup servings.

STRAWBERRY BOWL

Fresh strawberries and champagne—what could be more festive?

1 quart fresh strawberries

½ cup superfine sugar

1 tablespoon lemon juice

1 bottle (⅘ quart) Rhine, Riesling, or Chablis wine

1 bottle (⅘ quart) champagne, chilled

2 cups sparkling water, chilled

Block of ice or ice ring

Rinse, then remove the hulls from the strawberries. Place in a punch bowl. Sprinkle with the sugar and lemon juice. Pour in half the bottle of wine (chill the remainder). Let stand at least 1 hour, but no more than 3 hours.

To serve, add the remainder of the wine, a block or ring of ice, the champagne, and the sparkling water; stir gently to blend.

Ladle into punch cups, including a few strawberries in each serving.

Makes about 3 quarts, or 24 punch-cup servings.

WHITE SANGRIA

Sangria is usually made with red wine and served from a pitcher during the summer. It makes a perfectly respectable punch for the holidays. This version, made with white wine, is garnished with slices of oranges, lemons, and apples.

2 oranges, cut in half and thinly sliced

2 lemons, cut in half and thinly sliced

2 red apples, cored and cut in thin wedges

1 cup brandy

¼ cup curaçao or other orange-flavored liqueur

1⅓ cups superfine sugar

1 gallon Chablis wine, chilled

2 quarts sparkling water, chilled

Block of ice or ice ring

Combine the fruits, brandy, curaçao, and sugar in a bowl. Let stand several hours at room temperature—the longer the better.

When ready to serve, turn the marinated fruits into a punch bowl. Stir in the wine, then the sparkling water.

Add a block of ice or an ice ring; serve immediately in punch cups, adding some fruit to each.

Makes about 6 quarts, or 48 punch-cup servings.

RUM PUNCH

An unusual punch made with tea, which seems to pull together and blend the flavors of the other ingredients.

1 **can (6 ounces) frozen orange juice concentrate, thawed**

1 **cup cold strong tea (method follows)**

2 **cups light rum**

1 **quart ginger ale, chilled**

1 **quart 7-Up, chilled**

Block of ice or ice ring

Combine the orange juice (not diluted), tea, and rum in a punch bowl. Add ice; then gently add and stir in the ginger ale and 7-Up. Serve in punch cups.

Makes about 3 quarts, or 24 punch-cup servings.

  Note: Large bottles of carbonated beverages are often 28 ounces rather than 32 and can be used here.

  To make the tea, use 2 tea bags for 1 cup boiling water; steep for 5 minutes.

BOMBAY PUNCH

This champagne punch is smooth and potent. It is best served in a bowl set in cracked ice to prevent weakening the potion.

1 quart cognac

1 quart medium-dry sherry

¾ cup cherry brandy

¾ cup Cointreau

4 bottles (⅘ quart each) dry champagne

1 quart sparkling water (optional)

Orange and lemon slices, for garnish

All of the ingredients should be prechilled.

Set a punch bowl in a larger container and surround with cracked ice.

Pour the cognac, sherry, cherry brandy, and Cointreau into the punch bowl; blend. Pour in the champagne (down the side of the bowl to prevent losing the bubbles) and the sparkling water (optional). Stir gently. Float orange and lemon slices on top.

Ladle into punch cups for serving.

Makes about 7 quarts, or 50 punch-cup servings.

WHISKEY CUP

Reminiscent of old-fashioneds and similarly garnished with maraschino cherries and orange slices.

1 **quart bourbon whiskey**

½ **cup grenadine (see note)**

¼ **cup sugar**

6 **tablespoons lemon juice**

1 **quart sparkling water, chilled**

Maraschino cherries and half orange slices, for garnish

Combine the whiskey and grenadine. Dissolve the sugar in the lemon juice, then add to the whiskey mixture. Refrigerate. (Can be made in advance and held as long as you like.)

When ready to serve, pour the whiskey mixture into a pitcher; gently stir in the sparkling water.

Pour over ice cubes in old-fashioned glasses. Garnish each serving with a maraschino cherry and a half slice of orange.

Makes about 2 quarts, or 16 servings.

Note: Grenadine is a sweet, red syrup made from the juice of pomegranates. It may be purchased in bottles in supermarkets.

PRESIDENT MADISON'S WHISKEY SOURS

This is an adaptation of a recipe said to have been served in the White House when James Madison was president.

- 2 cups water
- ⅔ cup sugar (about)
- 8 lemons, juice and rinds
- 1 quart bourbon whiskey
- Orange slices, cut in half
- Maraschino cherries

Bring the water and ⅔ cup of sugar to a boil, stirring until the sugar is dissolved. Add the lemon rinds (no juice), then simmer 3 minutes. Cool, pour into a nonmetallic bowl.

Stir in the lemon juice and bourbon. Taste and add more sugar if required. Refrigerate at least 12 hours. Then remove the rinds and squeeze them dry. (If not serving immediately, return to refrigerator.)

Serve in whiskey sour glasses, or other cocktail glasses. Garnish each with a slice of orange and a maraschino cherry. *Makes about 2 quarts, or 20 cocktail servings.*

ONE-TWO-THREE DAIQUIRIS

An easy formula: one can frozen limeade, two cans rum, and three cans of water. Although the mixture is placed in the freezer, it will not freeze solidly; it merely becomes icy.

1 can (12 ounces) frozen limeade concentrate, thawed

2 cans light rum (limeade can used as measure)

3 cans water (limeade can)

Slices of fresh lime, for garnish (optional)

Combine the limeade (do not dilute), rum, and water in a bowl. Freeze for at least 24 hours before serving.

When ready to serve, stir briskly with a whisk; then spoon into cocktail glasses or punch cups. Garnish each with a slice of lime (optional).

Makes 2 quarts, or 18 4-ounce servings.

SCOTCH SOURS

Similar to the previous recipe in that a fruit juice concentrate can is used as a measure. This one is mixed in a blender.

1 can (6 ounces) frozen lemonade concentrate, thawed

1 can Scotch whisky (lemonade can as measure)

1 can sparkling water (lemonade can)

1 can cold water (lemonade can)

Turn the lemonade into the container of a blender. Add the Scotch, sparkling water, and cold water; blend until smooth. Serve over ice cubes in old-fashioned glasses.

Makes 4 to 6 servings.

Note: Make 2 or 3 times the recipe in advance, if desired; chill.

PERFECT BLOODY MARYS

Perfect Bloody Marys, extra spicy. You may wish to reduce the amounts of Worcestershire and Tabasco to your own taste—or that of your guests.

  1 **can (46 ounces) tomato juice**

  2 **cups vodka**

  ¾ **cup lemon juice**

  1 **teaspoon salt**

  4 **tablespoons Worcestershire sauce**

  1 **teaspoon Tabasco sauce**

  Celery sticks, for garnish (optional)

Combine the tomato juice, vodka, lemon juice, and salt. Stir in the Worcestershire sauce and Tabasco. Chill.

Stir well again before serving. Serve over ice cubes in doubles glasses. Insert a tall, thin celery stick in each.
Makes about 10 servings.

CHRISTMAS BREADS

Christmas sweet yeast breads are represented by European favorites such as German Dresden Stollen, rich with butter and chock-full of fruits and nuts; fragrant Cardamom Braid, formed from a single braid of dough; and Bohemian Houska, which is made in a tier with three braids; Potica, a Polish bread ring with a poppy seed filling; and the light and airy Italian Panettone. Among the tea breads, which are made without yeast, are simple French Spiced Bread with anise flavor; Bishop's Bread, which includes chocolate bits among the fruits and nuts; and old-fashioned Brown Bread baked in food cans.

31

NORWEGIAN JULEKAGE

A round, shiny brown loaf, containing raisins and citron. The predominant flavor comes from cardamom, a spice commonly used in the Scandinavian countries.

1 package dry yeast

¼ cup warm water (110°)

¾ cup milk

2 tablespoons butter

½ cup sugar

1 teaspoon salt

1 teaspoon ground cardamom (see note)

1 egg, slightly beaten

½ cup dark raisins, chopped

½ cup diced citron or candied lemon peel, chopped

3 to 3¼ cups unsifted all-purpose flour

1 egg yolk blended with 2 tablespoons cold water, for glaze

Sprinkle the yeast over the warm water in a measuring cup. Stir to dissolve.

Heat the milk and butter in a saucepan just until the butter melts. Pour into a large mixing bowl; stir in the sugar, salt, and cardamom; cool to lukewarm.

Stir in the yeast mixture. Add the egg, raisins, citron, and 2 cups of the flour. Beat with a wooden spoon until smooth.

Add just enough of the remaining flour (about 1 cup) to

32

make a soft dough that can be handled easily. (Use your hand or a spoon for mixing.)

Turn out onto a lightly floured board. Knead until smooth and elastic, about 10 minutes, adding only enough additional flour to keep the dough from sticking.

Place the dough in a large greased bowl, turning to bring the greased side up. Cover with a towel. Let rise in a warm place (85°) until doubled in volume, 1½ to 2 hours.

Punch down; let rise again, covered, until doubled, about 45 minutes. Shape into a round loaf; place in a greased 8-inch round layer cake pan. Cover and let rise again, about 45 minutes.

Brush with the egg yolk glaze. Bake in a preheated 350° oven for 30 to 40 minutes. Remove to a rack for cooling.

Makes 1 large loaf.

Note: Grinding seed from cardamom pods is preferable to that purchased already ground. See p. 37 for Cardamom Braid.

ITALIAN PANETTONE

Panettone is the traditional Christmas bread of Italy. It is a light bread baked into round loaves with a symbolic cross cut into the top. A glass of sweet wine is a favorite accompaniment.

2 packages dry yeast

1 teaspoon sugar

¼ cup warm water (110°)

½ cup (1 stick) butter

¾ cup cold milk

½ cup sugar

1 teaspoon salt

7 egg yolks (at room temperature), lightly beaten

5 to 5½ cups unsifted all-purpose flour

½ cup light raisins

½ cup dark raisins

½ cup citron, cut in thin slivers

¼ cup melted butter

Sprinkle the yeast and the 1 teaspoon of sugar over the warm water. Let stand a few minutes, then stir until dissolved. Let stand again another few minutes, or until quite foamy.

Melt the butter in a large saucepan. Add the cold milk, which will cool it to lukewarm. Add the ½ cup of sugar, salt, and beaten egg yolks; then stir in the dissolved yeast.

Add enough flour to make a very soft, sticky dough, about 4½ cups.

Turn out onto a lightly floured board and knead until smooth and elastic, kneading in as much of the remaining 1 cup flour as needed. (The dough should be soft; kneading will take about 10 minutes.)

Shape the dough into a ball and place in a greased bowl. Turn to bring the greased surface to the top. Cover with a towel and let rise in a warm place (85°) until doubled in bulk, about 2 hours.

Turn the dough out onto a board and knead in the raisins and citron (handle the dough as little as possible). Divide and shape into 2 balls.

Place one in each of the two prepared pans (see directions below). Cut a deep cross on top of each loaf, using a sharp knife. Let rise again until almost doubled, about 1 hour.

Brush the tops of the loaves with a little of the melted butter. Bake in a preheated 350° oven (middle shelf) for 30 to 40 minutes. When done the tops should be crisp and dark brown.

Remove from the pans to cooling racks. Brush again with butter (this will soften the crust). Cool, then strip off the paper.

Cut into thick wedges for serving.

Makes 2 tall loaves.

To prepare the pans, you will need two 8-inch round layer cake pans. Cut two strips of heavy brown paper (grocery sacks) into 20 × 5-inch lengths. Butter one side generously and fit inside (greased side in) the edge of the pan, over-lapping the ends. Use paper clips to hold in place.

CARDAMOM BRAID

An easily made single braided loaf. No fruits, no nuts—only cardamom for flavor.

    1   package dry yeast
    ¼   cup warm water (110°)
    ½   cup milk
    ⅓   cup sugar
    4   tablespoons (½ stick) butter
    ½   teaspoon salt
    2   teaspoons ground cardamom (see note)
    2¾ to 3 cups sifted all-purpose flour
    1   egg
        Milk and 1½ tablespoons sugar, for glaze

Sprinkle the yeast over the warm water in a measuring cup. Stir to dissolve.

Heat the milk in a large saucepan until bubbles appear around the edge. Remove from the heat and add the sugar, butter, and salt. Stir until the butter melts; cool to lukewarm.

Blend the cardamom into 1 cup of the flour; add to the milk mixture; mix well. Stir in the egg and the yeast mixure. Beat well. Add enough of the remaining flour (1¾ to 2 cups) to make a soft dough.

Turn out onto a lightly floured surface. Cover and let rest 10 minutes. Then knead until smooth and elastic, 8 to 10 minutes.

Place in a lightly greased bowl, turning once to grease the

surface. Cover; let rise in a warm place (85°) until doubled in bulk, about 1¼ hours. Punch down. Then let rise again until almost doubled, about 1 hour.

Turn the dough out onto a floured surface; divide into thirds and form into balls. Cover; let rest 10 minutes.

Using your hands, roll each ball into a strand 16 inches long, tapering the ends. Line them up on a greased baking sheet 1 inch apart. Braid loosely (without stretching the dough), beginning in the middle, and working toward one end, then the other. Pinch the ends together and fold under. Cover and let rise until almost doubled, about 40 minutes.

Just before baking, brush the braid with milk and sprinkle with the 1½ tablespoons of sugar.

Bake in a preheated 350° oven about 35 minutes, or until done.

Makes 1 large braided loaf.

Note: Although ground cardamom can be purchased, buying seed pods and grinding your own will provide a more fragrant product. (Both are available in stores that specialize in Scandinavian or Indian products.) The pods are papery thin and need to be split to remove the seeds. Grind, using a mortar and pestle, until fine.

HOUSKA

A triple-tiered braided Bohemian loaf garnished with sliced almonds.
Something of a challenge to make, but beautiful when skillfully done.

   2 packages dry yeast

  ¼ cup warm water (110°)

  1 cup milk

  ¾ cup sugar

  ½ cup (1 stick) butter

  2 eggs

     Grated rind of 1 lemon

  ¼ teaspoon nutmeg, freshly grated

  1 teaspoon salt

5½ cups sifted all-purpose flour (about)

  ¼ cup raisins

  ¼ cup citron, chopped

  1 egg mixed with 1 tablespoon water, for glaze

  ¼ cup blanched almonds, chopped

  ¼ cup sliced unblanched almonds, for garnish

Sprinkle the yeast over the warm water in a measuring cup.
Stir to dissolve.

Scald the milk. Pour over the sugar and butter, which
have been placed in the bowl of an electric mixer. Cool to
lukewarm.

Add the eggs, grated lemon rind, nutmeg, salt, yeast mixture, and 3 cups of the flour. Beat until smooth. Add the

raisins, citron, and almonds; mix well. Add enough of the remaining flour to make a soft dough. Turn out onto a lightly floured board and knead until satiny, about 10 minutes.

Place in a greased bowl; turn greased side up, then cover, and let rise in a warm place (85°) until double in bulk, about 1 hour and 15 minutes.

Punch the dough down; turn it out onto a lightly floured board and knead briefly. Divide the dough in half. Divide one half into 3 equal parts; using your hands, roll each on a lightly floured surface, into a strand about 18 inches long, tapering the ends. Line up on a greased baking sheet 1 inch apart. Braid loosely, beginning in the middle and working toward one end; then braid the other end. Pinch the ends together and fold under.

Divide two-thirds of the remaining dough into 3 equal parts. Form a second braid (slightly shorter) and place on top of the first one. Repeat with the remaining dough and place on top of the second braid.

Cover and let rise until double in bulk (about 1 hour). Brush the top with the egg mixed with the water. Sprinkle with the sliced almonds.

Bake in a preheated 350° oven for 40 to 45 minutes, or until golden brown. Cool.

Makes one triple-braided loaf.

DRESDEN STOLLEN

German Dresden Stollen, perhaps the most famous of all Christmas breads, is made from a rich dough generously filled with raisins, candied fruit peels, and almonds. The loaf is crescent-shaped and is coated with powdered sugar.

3 packages dry yeast

2 cups lukewarm milk (90°)

1 cup sugar

8 cups unsifted all-purpose flour (about)

1 pound (4 sticks) butter, softened

4 eggs

1 teaspoon salt

   Grated rind of 1 lemon

1 cup light raisins

½ cup currants

½ cup diced candied citron, cut fine

½ cup diced candied orange peel, cut fine

1 cup blanched almonds, chopped

   Melted butter

   Confectioners' sugar

Combine the yeast with ⅓ cup of the lukewarm milk, 2 tablespoons of the sugar, and 2 tablespoons of the flour. Set aside to rise until foamy.

Cream the butter with the remaining sugar until light. Add the eggs, one at a time, beating well after each addition. Beat in the salt and grated lemon rind.

blend in the yeast mixture. Add the remaining lukewarm milk alternately with the remaining flour, adding just enough flour to make a soft dough. Turn out onto a floured board and knead until smooth and elastic.

Sprinkle a little flour over the raisins, currants, citron, and orange peel; mix well. Knead into the dough along with the almonds.

Place the dough in a lightly greased bowl, turning to bring the greased side up. Cover and let rise in a warm place (85°) until doubled, about 1½ hours.

Divide the dough into 3 equal portions; roll each to about a 16 × 8-inch oval; brush with melted butter. Press lengthwise down the center with a rolling pin. Then fold in half, bringing one side to within one half inch of the opposite edge. Press the fold lightly.

Place the stollen on a lightly greased baking sheet. Brush the tops with melted butter. Let rise again until light, about 45 minutes. (Stollen will not double.)

Bake in a preheated 350° oven for about 45 minutes, or until golden brown. Remove to racks for cooling. While hot, brush again with melted butter and sprinkle well with confectioners' sugar. Cool. Just before serving, sprinkle again with the sugar to coat.

Makes 3 stollen.

CHRISTOLLEN

This German Christmas bread has its counterpart in many countries of Europe. The fragrant, fruit-filled pinwheel loaf befits a special occasion.

1 cup (2 sticks) butter

1 cup milk

½ cup water

5¼ cups sifted all-purpose flour

¼ cup sugar

1 teaspoon salt

2 packages dry yeast

2 eggs, beaten

½ teaspoon orange rind, grated

½ teaspoon lemon rind, grated

½ cup raisins (light or dark)

½ cup candied fruit, chopped (preferably cherries and pineapple)

½ cup nuts, chopped

4 tablespoons butter, melted

½ cup sugar mixed with 1 tablespoon cinnamon
Confectioners' Sugar Glaze (recipe follows)
Candied cherry halves and finely chopped nuts, for garnish

Melt the butter in a small saucepan. Stir in the milk and water; heat until lukewarm.

Combine the flour, sugar, salt, and yeast in a large mixing bowl. Stir in the milk mixture and beaten eggs; mix well.

Add the orange and lemon rinds, raisins, candied fruit, and nuts; mix well.

Turn the dough into a greased bowl; turn to bring the greased side up. Cover and refrigerate overnight.

Place the chilled dough on a floured surface. Roll into an 18 × 12-inch rectangle. Spread with 3 tablespoons of the melted butter. Sprinkle with the sugar and cinnamon mixture.

Roll up tightly, beginning at the wide end. Moisten the edge of the dough with water; pinch edges together to seal well.

Place the roll, sealed edge down, on a greased baking sheet, joining the ends to form a ring; moisten and pinch together. With scissors, cut two-thirds of the way through the outer edge at 1-inch intervals. Turn each cut section on its side, overlapping slightly.

Brush the ring with the remaining 1 tablespoon of melted butter. Cover and let rise about 1 hour.

Bake in a preheated 350° oven for 25 to 30 minutes.

While still warm, dribble the Confectioners' Sugar Glaze over the top. Decorate with the cherry halves and chopped nuts.

Makes 1 decorative wreath.

CONFECTIONERS' SUGAR GLAZE

1 cup sifted confectioners' sugar

¼ teaspoon vanilla extract

2 to 3 tablespoons milk

Combine the sugar, vanilla, and enough milk to make a thin glaze.

POTICA

Potica (po-TEET-za) is the Polish version of a light yeast bread baked in a ring. Each slice contains a swirl of poppy seed filling, which, with a striated sugar frosting, makes a serving of unusual interest.

1 **cake compressed yeast (see note)**

2 **tablespoons lukewarm water (90°)**

¼ **cup sugar**

6 **tablespoons milk**

2½ **tablespoons butter**

½ **teaspoon salt**

2 **egg yolks, beaten**

2 **cups plus 2 tablespoons sifted all-purpose flour**

Poppy Seed Filling (recipe follows)

Glaze (recipe follows)

Crumble the yeast into the lukewarm water. Stir in ½ teaspoon of the sugar and let soften 10 minutes.

Combine the remaining sugar, milk, butter, and salt in a saucepan. Heat and stir until the sugar is dissolved. Pour into a mixing bowl and cool to lukewarm. Stir in the yeast mixture and the beaten egg yolks.

Add 1 cup of the flour and beat hard with a wire whisk.

Gradually stir in 1 cup more flour; stir until well mixed. Cover, let stand 10 minutes; then turn out onto a board sprinkled with the remaining 2 tablespoons of flour. Knead thoroughly, at least 5 minutes. (The dough is soft, but its richness prevents it from adhering to the board if the kneading is done fast. The dough must be soft to make a light and flaky coffee cake.)

Note: You may substitute 1 package dry yeast. Dissolve in warm water (110°).

44

Place the dough in a lightly greased bowl; turn once to bring the greased side up. Cover with a damp cloth and let rise in a warm place (85°) until doubled.

Punch down, turn over, cover and let rise again until doubled. Punch down and turn onto a lightly floured board; cover with the bowl and let rest 10 minutes.

Roll the dough into a 12 × 16-inch rectangle. Spread with Poppy Seed Filling to within one inch of the edges. Roll up like a jelly roll from the long side and pinch the ends and sides to seal.

Place seam side down on a greased baking sheet, bringing the ends together to form a ring. Cover and let rise until light. Bake in a preheated 350° oven for 25 to 30 minutes.

When slightly cool, drizzle the Glaze over the top, from side to side around the ring.

Makes 1 filled ring.

POPPY SEED FILLING

- 1 **cup poppy seeds**
- ½ **cup sugar**
- ½ **cup milk**
- 2 **tablespoons butter**

Combine the poppy seeds, sugar, milk, and butter in a saucepan. Cook, stirring until the mixture thickens, about 10 minutes. Cool.

GLAZE

- 1 **teaspoon butter**
- 2 **teaspoons water**
- ½ **cup sifted confectioners' sugar**

Melt the butter with the water; stir in the confectioners' sugar.

DANISH KRINGLE

Thin layers of dough enclose a honey and walnut mixture, forming a delightful glazed sandwich. The dough is mixed like pie crust and requires no kneading.

4 cups sifted all-purpose flour

3 tablespoons sugar

1 teaspoon salt

1 cup (2 sticks) butter

1 cup milk

1 package dry yeast

3 eggs, separated

1 cup brown sugar (packed)

1 cup walnuts, ground

¼ cup honey

¼ cup melted butter

Glaze (recipe follows)

Sift the flour, sugar, and salt into a large bowl. Cut in the butter, using a pastry blender, as for pie crust.

Heat the milk until warm (110°); sprinkle in the yeast; stir to dissolve. Beat the egg yolks; add to the milk and yeast; then add to the flour mixture; mix well. Scrape down the sides of the bowl. Cover with waxed paper, then with a damp towel. Refrigerate overnight.

Grease a 15 × 10-inch jelly roll pan. Divide the dough into two equal parts. Roll out one half on a lightly floured surface to fit the pan (including sides). Place in the bottom of the pan and work up against the sides.

46

Beat the egg whites until almost stiff; spread over the dough. Combine the brown sugar and the walnuts; sprinkle over the dough. Drizzle the honey and the melted butter over the top.

Roll out the remaining dough (to the same size) and place on top of the filling. Pinch edges together. Let rise covered in a warm place for 30 minutes.

Bake in a preheated 350° oven for about 30 minutes. Cool a few minutes; then spread the top with the Glaze. When cold cut in squares to serve.

Makes 1 large coffee cake.

GLAZE

> 1 **cup sifted confectioners' sugar**
>
> 1 **tablespoon milk**
>
> ¼ **teaspoon vanilla extract**

Combine the sugar, milk, and vanilla.

SALLY LUNN

An easily made batter bread (no kneading), which is best served fresh and warm with butter.

1 cup milk

¼ cup water

½ cup (1 stick) butter

4 cups sifted all-purpose flour

⅓ cup sugar

2 teaspoons salt

2 packages dry yeast

3 eggs

Heat the milk, water, and butter until very warm (about 120°).

In a bowl of an electric mixer, place 1⅓ cups of the flour, sugar, salt, and yeast. Stir well. Gradually add the warm liquid mixture; beat at low speed for 2 minutes, scraping down the sides occasionally. Add the eggs and 1⅓ cups more flour; beat at medium speed for 2 minutes. Remove from the mixer and stir in the remaining 1⅓ cups flour with a wooden spoon.

Cover and let rise in a warm place until doubled in bulk, 1 to 1½ hours. Stir the dough down and turn into a well greased 10-inch tube or Bundt pan. Cover and let rise again until almost doubled.

Bake in a preheated 350° oven for about 40 minutes, or until golden brown and crusty. Let stand a few minutes, then turn out. The bread is very crusty, but somewhat fragile. Use a serrated knife for cutting.

Best served slightly warm with butter.

Makes 1 large loaf.

FRENCH SPICED BREAD

A simple loaf bread intriguingly flavored with honey and anise.

2 cups sifted all-purpose flour

1 teaspoon baking powder

½ teaspoon baking soda

½ teaspoon salt

½ cup honey

½ cup sugar

1 cup boiling water

½ teaspoon anise extract

Sift flour, baking powder, baking soda, and salt together three times.

Measure the honey and sugar into a mixing bowl; add the boiling water; stir until the sugar is dissolved. While the mixture is hot, add the flour mixture (all at one time); then add the anise extract. Beat well with a wire whisk or spoon until smooth.

Turn into a greased 9 × 5 × 3-inch loaf pan. Bake in a preheated 375° oven for about 40 minutes. Cool.

Slice thin for serving.

Makes 1 loaf.

BISHOP'S BREAD

A holiday loaf from New England, gay and colorful with Christmas fruit and tidbits of chocolate.

1½ cups sifted all-purpose flour

1½ teaspoons baking powder

½ teaspoon salt

1 package (6 ounces) semisweet chocolate morsels

2 cups walnuts, broken

1 cup dried apricots, chopped

1 cup candied cherries, halved

3 eggs

1 cup sugar

Sift the flour with the baking powder and salt into a mixing bowl. Stir in the chocolate morsels, walnuts, apricots, and cherries.

Beat the eggs in a separate mixing bowl. Then gradually beat in the sugar. Fold in the flour mixture.

Line the bottom of a 9 × 5 × 3-inch loaf pan with waxed paper; grease the paper and sides of the pan. Turn the mixture into the loaf pan. Spread evenly.

Bake in a preheated 325° oven for about 1 hour and 30 minutes, or until done. Cool in the pan on a wire rack. Remove, invert, and wrap when cool. (It will keep for days.)
Makes 1 loaf.

CRANBERRY LOAF

Fresh cranberries, orange juice, orange peel, and walnuts give flavor, color, and texture to this easily made Christmas bread.

1¼ cups fresh cranberries

1 cup sugar

2 cups sifted all-purpose flour

1½ teaspoons baking powder

½ teaspoon baking soda

1 teaspoon salt

½ cup walnuts, coarsely chopped

1 egg

¾ cup orange juice

2 teaspoons orange rind, grated

2 tablespoons butter, melted

Rinse and drain the cranberries. Cut into halves with scissors. Mix with ¼ cup of the sugar.

Sift the flour, the remaining ¾ cup sugar, baking powder, baking soda, and salt into a mixing bowl. Add the walnuts and the sugared cranberries; mix well.

Beat the egg lightly. Stir in the orange juice, orange rind, and the melted butter. Make a well in the center of the dry ingredients and add the orange juice mixture. Mix only enough to moisten the dry ingredients.

Turn into a 9 × 5 × 3-inch loaf pan, which has been greased on the bottom and then lined with waxed paper. Bake in a preheated 350° oven for 40 to 45 minutes.

Remove from the oven and run a spatula gently around the sides of the pan. Turn the bread out and peel off the waxed paper. Cool upright on a rack. Wrap securely when cold.
Makes 1 loaf.

TOASTED COCONUT BREAD

An unusual and delicious tea loaf. Toasted coconut separates it from other similar breads.

3 cups sifted all-purpose flour

1 cup sugar

3 teaspoons baking powder

½ teaspoon salt

1 cup shredded coconut, toasted (method follows)

1 egg

1½ cups milk

1 teaspoon vanilla extract

Sift the flour with the sugar, baking powder, and salt. Stir in the toasted coconut.

Beat the egg until foamy; stir in the milk and vanilla. Add to the dry ingredients; mix thoroughly but do not beat.

Pour into a lightly greased 9 × 5 × 3-inch loaf pan. Bake in a preheated 325° oven for 60 to 70 minutes, or until a pick inserted in the center comes out clean.

Cool 10 minutes, then turn out and cool on a rack. Wrap and refrigerate a day before serving. Cut into thin slices. *Makes 1 loaf.*

To toast the coconut, spread it in a shallow pan. Bake in a preheated 350° oven, turning frequently to brown evenly, for about 12 to 15 minutes until dry and golden. Cool.

BROWN BREAD

An old-fashioned bread baked in empty fruit cans. Especially good when sliced and spread with cream cheese.

2½ cups unsifted all-purpose flour

2½ cups 40% Bran Flakes

1 cup dark raisins

1 teaspoon baking soda

1 egg

¾ cup sugar

1 cup dark corn syrup

2 cups buttermilk

Mix together the flour, bran flakes, raisins, and baking soda.

Combine the egg, sugar, corn syrup, and buttermilk, mixing until well blended. Stir into the flour mixture; mix well.

Pour the batter into 4 well-greased and floured No. 2 cans (20 ounces or 2½ cup capacity). Bake in a preheated 375° oven about 1 hour, or until a cake tester comes out clean. Cool in the cans. Wrap to store (may be frozen).

Makes 3 tall round loaves.

Note: Smaller cans may be substituted; fill only three-quarters full and use tester for length of baking time.

COLD CANAPES, DIPS AND SPREADS

Among the cold appetizers are such easily made dips and spreads as Tangy Blue Cheese Dip; herb-flavored Pâté Beau Monde; colorful Red Caviar with Sour Cream; and Tapenade, a savory, creamy tuna dip served with crisp raw vegetables. There are Little Turkey Sandwiches, a party canapé with edges attractively rolled in chopped almonds and parsley; piquant, deviled Lemon Eggs; Icelandic Shrimp Mold with half as many shrimp scattered over the top as there are in the spread itself; and a superb aspic-glazed chicken liver pâté, elegantly presented with a tomato rose garnish.

LEMON EGGS

A delicately flavored version of deviled eggs. The filling is lightly accented with lemon juice and rind—perfect for a holiday party.

6 **large eggs, hard cooked (see note)**

3 **tablespoons mayonnaise**

Juice of 1 lemon (2 tablespoons)

Rind of 1 lemon, finely grated

¼ **teaspoon (scant) dry mustard**

3 **dashes Tabasco sauce**

½ **teaspoon salt**

Flat Italian parsley leaflets, for garnish

Cut the shelled eggs lengthwise into halves. Gently scoop out the yolks into a small mixing bowl. Mash them with a fork until smooth. Blend in the mayonnaise, lemon juice and rind, mustard, Tabasco sauce, and salt.

Spoon the mixture into the cavities of the egg whites, mounding lightly. Cover and refrigerate, but for better flavor remove long enough before serving to bring close to room temperature. Garnish each filled egg with a tiny leaflet of parsley, placed at the wide end of the white, at the edge of the filling. (A simple but attractive garnish.)

Makes 12 filled egg halves.

Note: The eggs must be perfectly cooked so that the whites are firm, not rubbery, and the yolks cooked through but without a tinge of green. Here is one way. Place refrigerated eggs in a saucepan large enough to hold them in one layer without crowding. Add cold water to cover by at least 1 inch. Bring to a rolling boil uncovered over high heat; then simmer, turning occasionally, 12 minutes longer. Drain off the water, then cover the eggs with cold water to fill the pan. Let stand until cool. Remove from the water, then crack the shells and peel. If not using immediately, refrigerate; shell when ready to use.

BENEDICTINE CANAPÉS

A pale green cucumber spread for rounds of fresh white bread.

1 **large cucumber**

½ **small onion**

1 **package (8 ounces) cream cheese, at room temperature**

1 **teaspoon (scant) salt**

Dash of Tabasco sauce

Mayonnaise

Few drops green food coloring

18 **slices white sandwich bread**

Tiny cucumber wedges and parsley leaflets, for garnish

Peel and seed the cucumber. Chop fine, along with the onion, in a food processor. Turn into a wire sieve and press to extract the excess juice. (Do not make too dry.)

Whip the cream cheese with a fork until smooth; then stir in the cucumber mixture, salt, and Tabasco sauce. Add just enough mayonnaise to make a soft spread. Add a few drops of food coloring to tint a *pale* green; blend well.

Cut the bread into rounds, using a 1½-inch cutter. (Stack them as they are cut and cover with damp paper towels to prevent drying.) You will need about 72 rounds.

Spread the tops of the bread rounds generously with the cream cheese mixture. Chill in pans, covered first with waxed paper, then with damp paper towels. (May be stored overnight.) Serve slightly chilled.

When ready to serve, or a few hours in advance, garnish the canapés as follows. Cut several slices from an unpeeled cucumber, about ⅛ inch thick. Cut small wedges from the sides (omitting the seeds); stand one wedge upright in the center of each canapé; then place a leaflet of parsley alongside. For serving, arrange the canapés on a dark wooden tray or other tray, which will give some contrast.

Makes about 6 dozen canapés.

LITTLE TURKEY SANDWICHES

Edges decorated with chopped almonds and parsley give special flair to these small, round party sandwiches. The filling is minced turkey—a great way to use leftovers.

  4 tablespoons soft butter

  1 cup cooked turkey or chicken, finely chopped

  1 tablespoon onion, finely chopped

  1½ tablespoons cream sherry

  ⅛ teaspoon salt

  ⅛ teaspoon celery salt

    Mayonnaise

  12 slices melba-thin white bread (must be fresh)

  ½ cup (rounded) sliced almonds, toasted and
     finely chopped (method follows)

  2 tablespoons parsley, finely chopped

Cream the butter in a small mixing bowl. Add the turkey (it must be finely chopped) and mash with a fork until well blended. Add the onion, sherry, salt, celery salt, and just enough mayonnaise to bind. Cover and refrigerate several hours to blend the flavors. Remove before using, so that the pâté is spreadable.

Cut the bread into rounds, using a 1½-inch cutter. Stack them as they are cut and cover with damp paper towels to prevent drying. You will need 48 rounds.

Spread half the rounds with the turkey pâté (about ¼-inch thick) and top with the remaining bread rounds. Run your finger around the sides to smooth any exposed filling. (Keep covered when possible.)

Spread a thin coating of mayonnaise on a small plate. Sprinkle the chopped almonds and parsley on a second plate; mix.

Holding one sandwich in your fingers like a wheel, run the edges lightly through the mayonnaise, then through the almond mixture.

Arrange on a platter and serve without chilling. (They may be prepared several hours in advance. Place in a cake pan with waxed paper between the layers and on top. Cover with damp paper towels. Chill if held long.)

Makes 24 tiny sandwiches.

To toast the almonds, place in a baking pan. Bake at 300°, stirring occasionally, until golden brown—about 15 minutes.

CREOLE SHRIMP RÉMOULADE

A New Orleans specialty. Recipes vary; all are good, but this is one of the best. The sauce requires a zesty Creole mustard.

2 pounds medium-size shrimp, peeled and cooked (method follows)

4 tablespoons Creole mustard (see note)

2 tablespoons cider vinegar

6 tablespoons olive oil

1 tablespoon paprika

½ teaspoon salt

½ teaspoon white pepper

1 tablespoon scallions, finely chopped

¼ cup parsley, finely chopped

¼ cup celery, finely chopped

Shredded lettuce, for garnish

Prepare the shrimp as directed. Combine the mustard and vinegar. Using a wire whisk, beat in the olive oil, paprika, salt, and pepper. Stir in the scallions, parsley, and celery.

Add the shrimp; turn in the sauce to coat. Refrigerate at least two hours, so that the sauce permeates the shrimp.

When ready to serve, mix the shrimp in the sauce again. Serve on a platter lined with shredded lettuce. Provide small serving plates and forks. The shrimp are especially good with saltines.

Makes 8 to 10 servings.

Note: Creole mustard is a grainy mustard available in many specialty food shops.

To cook the shrimp: Peel and devein the shrimp. Place them in a 3-quart saucepan; add enough cold water to come up about 1 inch above the shrimp. Add 2 slices of lemon and 1 tablespoon salt. Bring the water to a boil, then simmer about 30 seconds. Remove from the heat and drain in a colander. Allow to cool; if not using immediately, cover to prevent drying.

WHITE CLAM DIP

A classic among clam dips—best served with potato chips.

1 clove garlic, peeled and cut in half

2 packages (3 ounces each) cream cheese, softened

1 teaspoon lemon juice

1 teaspoon Worcestershire sauce

2 tablespoons sour cream

1 tablespoon onion, grated

½ teaspoon salt, or to taste

1 can (6 ounces) minced clams

Potato chips

Rub the inside of a small mixing bowl with the garlic. Add the cream cheese, lemon juice, Worcestershire sauce, sour cream, onion, and salt; blend until smooth.

Drain the clams, reserving the juice. (If they are unevenly chopped, pick over and cut the larger ones into pieces.) Add to the cream cheese mixture. Stir in enough of the reserved clam juice to make a thin consistency for dipping. Chill several hours to blend the flavors.

Serve cold with potato chips for dipping.
Makes about 1⅓ cups.

Note: When adding the clam juice, use enough to make the mixture extra thin; it will firm when chilled.

TANGY BLUE CHEESE DIP

An olympic champion of the blue cheese dip competition. Stick pretzels are a must.

    2 packages (3 ounces each) cream cheese, at room temperature
½ cup mayonnaise
½ small onion
1 teaspoon Worcestershire sauce
2 ounces blue cheese
    Pretzel sticks

Mash the cream cheese with a fork in a small mixing bowl. Add the mayonnaise; blend until smooth. Grate the onion into the mixture, using the medium cutting edge of the grater. Add the Worcestershire sauce; blend.

Crumble the blue cheese into the cream cheese mixture, using your fingers. Then blend again with a fork until thoroughly mixed. (The mixture should be slightly lumpy, not smooth.) Turn into a serving bowl; cover and refrigerate several hours to blend the flavors.

Serve cold with thin pretzel sticks for dipping, the preferred accompaniment for this dip.

Makes about 1½ cups.

Note: Leftovers keep well, unless held too long at room temperature, as the mixture eventually becomes oily.

TAPENADE WITH CRUDITÉS

A smooth and creamy tuna dip for raw vegetables—a famous and old favorite from the kitchens of Provence. A food processor brings it easily to the American table.

1 can (6½ ounces) chunk light tuna in oil

¼ cup onion, chopped

¼ cup mayonnaise

Juice of 1 lemon (2 tablespoons)

½ teaspoon anchovy paste (or 1 canned anchovy)

5 large capers

2 sprigs fresh parsley leaves

2 slices white bread (crusts removed), cubed

¼ teaspoon salt

Dash of pepper

Crudités (see note)

Place the tuna with the oil in a food processor. Add the onion, mayonnaise, lemon juice, anchovy paste, capers, parsley, bread cubes, salt, and pepper. Blend until smooth, about 20 seconds. Scrape down the sides of the container with a spatula; blend again a few seconds longer. Chill before serving.

For a special presentation, serve the dip in a ceramic container; garnish with a sprig of parsley and two carrot sticks. Set in the center of a wooden tray and ring with the crudités.
Makes about 1½ cups.

Note: The raw vegetables (crudités) best suited for this dip are zucchini, carrots, celery, and turnips. They should be peeled, cut into convenient strips for dipping, then soaked in salted water (1 teaspoon to 1 quart water) with ice cubes, for at least 30 minutes; drain well.

PÂTÉ BEAU MONDE

This herb cheese spread has a tantalizing flavor. Superb on crackers—Triscuits are best—or as a filling for crisp celery.

2 packages (3 ounces each) cream cheese, at room temperature

1 tablespoon water

2½ teaspoons Beau Monde seasoning salt (see note)

¼ teaspoon dried thyme

¼ teaspoon dried marjoram

¼ teaspoon dried summer savory

1 tablespoon fresh parsley, finely chopped

Triscuits or celery sticks

Blend the cream cheese with the water and seasoning salt. Crush the dried herbs by rubbing between the palms of your hands; add the herbs along with the parsley. Stir the mixture until smooth. Chill several hours to blend the flavors.

Serve with Triscuits for spreading, or use to fill celery sticks.

Makes about ¾ cup.

Note: Beau Monde seasoning salt is a Spice Islands product, which is available in most supermarkets. The recipe is an adaptation of one printed on a company pamphlet more than 25 years ago.

GOLDEN EGG SPREAD

A light and airy blend of chopped hard-cooked eggs and cream cheese, with enough onion to give it bite.

    6 hard-cooked eggs
    ¼ cup onion, finely chopped
    2 packages (3 ounces each) cream cheese
    2 tablespoons (or more) rendered chicken fat (see note)
 1½ teaspoons salt
    ⅛ teaspoon white pepper (or to taste)
       Salty black olives, for garnish
       Party rye bread or pumpernickel

Slice the eggs into a mixing bowl; add the onion. Using a pastry blender, chop the eggs until the whites are not discernible from the yolks.

In a separate bowl, beat the cream cheese until creamy. Blend in 2 tablespoons of the chicken fat, the salt, and pepper. Add the eggs and mix lightly with a fork. Add a little more chicken fat if necessary to bind the mixture.

Pile into a shallow serving dish and ring the edge with black olives. (A single radish rose on top will enhance the appearance.) Serve at a cool room temperature with party rye bread or pumpernickel and a knife for spreading.

Makes 2 cups.

Note: Rendered chicken fat may be purchased in many supermarkets at the meat counter.

TOASTED ALMOND AND
CHEESE SPREAD

This butter-colored spread has a crunchy texture from chopped almonds and crisp bacon.

⅓ cup unblanched almonds

4 ounces Monterey Jack cheese, grated (see note)

½ cup mayonnaise

2 tablespoons onion, finely chopped

3 thin strips bacon

Party crackers (like Ritz)

Place the almonds in a single layer in a dry, heavy skillet. Stir over low heat until browned. Remove from the heat and cool. Chop coarsely. (It is impossible to do this evenly by hand or with a machine. Part will be coarse, part fine; use all.) Set aside 1 tablespoon for garnish.

Combine the cheese, mayonnaise, and onion in a mixing bowl. Add the almonds.

Fry the bacon until crisp; drain on paper towels. Then crumble over the cheese mixture. Blend in with a fork.

Pile the mixture into a small serving container and garnish with the remaining almonds. Chill covered until ready to serve. Serve with crackers for spreading.

This spread may be made several days in advance. The crisp bacon will soften, but will not be noticeable because of the crunch of the almonds.

Makes about 1½ cups.

Note: Monterey Jack is a semisoft light-colored cheese similar in flavor to Muenster, which is a good substitute.

POTTED JACK CHEESE

A California specialty made with Monterey Jack, a soft, creamy white cheese.

½ pound Monterey Jack cheese, grated

4 ounces chive cream cheese

¼ cup dry vermouth

2 teaspoons Dijon mustard

Party crackers or Melba Toast

Bring the Monterey Jack cheese and cream cheese to room temperature. Place in a mixing bowl. Add the vermouth and mustard. Beat with an electric mixer until smooth.

Pack into a cheese crock; cover and refrigerate. (Keeps well up to 3 weeks.)

Bring to room temperature before serving with crackers or Melba Toast.

Makes about 1½ cups.

RED CAVIAR WITH SOUR CREAM

Simple, elegant—and expensive.

> 2 jars (4 ounces each) salmon roe caviar
>
> 1 cup sour cream
>
> 4 thin scallions (white part only), thinly sliced
>
> 1/8 teaspoon Tabasco sauce
>
> 1/2 teaspoon lemon rind, grated
>
> 1 teaspoon lemon juice
>
> Pumpernickel or rye bread

Put the caviar in a strainer; dip up and down a few times in a bowl of cold water to remove the milky substance; drain thoroughly.

Set aside about a teaspoon of the caviar and a few green rings from the scallion tops for garnish. Then combine the remainder of the caviar with the sour cream, scallions, Tabasco, lemon rind, and lemon juice. (Mix gently as the caviar should remain whole.) Refrigerate until ready to serve.

Spoon the mixture into a serving dish and garnish the top with the reserved caviar and a scattering of the onion tops. Serve as a spread for pumpernickel or rye bread.

Makes about 2 cups.

Note: For an elegant presentation, which the dip deserves, spoon into a silver compote. Surround with the bread, cut in small pieces.

CRABMEAT COCKTAIL SPREAD

An unusual and attractive appetizer made in layers: cream cheese, crabmeat, cocktail sauce, and chopped parsley. The appearance is enhanced when served in a shallow glass compote.

1 package (6 ounces) frozen crabmeat

1 package (8 ounces) cream cheese, at room temperature

1 teaspoon onion, finely grated

½ cup chili sauce

1 tablespoon ketchup

1 teaspoon horseradish

½ teaspoon Worcestershire sauce

2 tablespoons lemon juice

1 bunch fresh parsley (leaflets only), finely chopped (see note)

Bremner Wafers or other crackers

Defrost the crabmeat. Place in a wire strainer set over a bowl to collect the juices. Pick over for any cartilage and shred the crabmeat coarsely with your fingers. Then press to extract the excess juices (it should be fairly dry). Set aside, reserving the juices.

Blend the cream cheese, onion, and just enough of the reserved crab juices (about 2 teaspoons) until smooth enough for spreading. Then spread over the bottom of a 9- to 10-inch shallow glass bowl or compote. (The mixture should be about ½ inch thick.) Top with the drained crabmeat, covering the mixture evenly. Refrigerate until ready to serve.

Combine the chili sauce, ketchup, horseradish, Worcestershire sauce, and lemon juice. Chill.

To serve, spread the chili sauce mixture evenly over the crabmeat. Sprinkle the parsley over the top, using just enough so that a little of the red sauce is visible. Serve immediately, with crackers for spreading.

Makes about 3 cups.

Note: To chop a large amount of parsley easily, pull off the leaflets. Drop into the container of a food processor or blender; cover generously with cold water. Process until finely chopped. Drain well; then press dry between several thicknesses of paper toweling.

SHRIMP MOUSSE

A ring mold or a fish mold is suitable for this elegant combination of shrimp and cream, delicately seasoned with tarragon. It is quickly prepared in a blender.

1 envelope unflavored gelatin

2 tablespoons lemon juice

1 thin slice of onion

½ cup boiling water

½ cup mayonnaise

2 cups cooked, shelled and deveined shrimp

¼ teaspoon paprika

1 teaspoon dried tarragon

1 cup heavy cream

Watercress sprigs, for garnish

Stoned Wheat Thins or other crackers

Pour the gelatin into the container of a blender. Add the lemon juice, onion, and the boiling water. Cover and blend on high for 40 seconds.

Add the mayonnaise, shrimp, paprika, and tarragon. Cover and blend on high until smooth. Then uncover, and, with the motor running, pour in the heavy cream; blend 30 seconds.

Pour into a lightly oiled 4-cup ring mold or fish mold. Chill until firm. Unmold, garnish with watercress sprigs, and serve with crackers. Stoned Wheat Thins are especially good with this.

Makes 4 cups.

ICELANDIC SHRIMP MOLD

A molded shrimp pâté served with a shower of tiny shrimp on top—
a beautiful presentation worthy of a special party.

2 **packages (6 ounces each) tiny frozen shrimp**
   (see note)

1½ **teaspoons dry mustard**

1 **teaspoon Worcestershire sauce**

2 **teaspoons lemon juice**

½ **cup mayonnaise (about)**

Parsley clusters

Cocktail Toast (method follows)

Defrost the shrimp according to package directions. Dry well between folds of paper toweling. Measure 2 cups of shrimp and refrigerate the remainder for a garnish.

Chop the 2 cups shrimp fine, almost to a paste, using a knife and cutting board (or use a food processor or blender). Place in a mixing bowl. Blend in the mustard, Worcestershire sauce, lemon juice, and enough mayonnaise to bind the mixture.

Line a small mixing bowl (2½- to 3-cup capacity) with plastic wrap. Pack the shrimp mixture firmly into the bowl and level the top. Refrigerate several hours or overnight.

To serve, unmold the shrimp mixture onto a serving plate. Scatter the remaining shrimp over the top. Use parsley clusters around the base for additional garnish. Serve with Cocktail Toast for spreading.

Makes about 3 cups.

Note: Most supermarkets sell tiny frozen shrimp. They are ¼ to ½ inch in diameter, and are shelled, deveined, and precooked.

COCKTAIL TOAST

Trim the crusts from firm textured sandwich bread. Spread lightly with sweet (unsalted) butter; cut each slice diagonally into quarters. Place on a baking sheet. Bake in a preheated 300° oven for about 30 minutes, or until golden brown and dry. Cool, then store tightly covered at room temperature until ready to serve. Keeps well for a week or more.

PÂTÉ D'ASCOT

The best chicken liver pâté you will ever taste. An elegant, smooth concoction with an aspic glaze and attractive tomato rose garnish.

  6 tablespoons butter

  1 medium onion, thinly sliced

  2 cloves garlic, put through a press

  2 pounds chicken livers, drained

  ¼ cup cognac

  2 teaspoons salt

  ¼ teaspoon white pepper

  ½ teaspoon dried tarragon, crushed

  1 cup heavy cream

     Aspic Glaze (method follows)

     Tomato Rose Garnish (method follows)

     Toasted French Bread Slices (method follows)

Melt 2 tablespoons of the butter in a large, heavy skillet. Add the onion and garlic. Sauté over low heat until the onion is very soft; do not brown.

Turn the heat to high. Add the whole chicken livers. Sauté, turning occasionally, until the livers are cooked through, but are still pink in the centers (about 7 minutes). Remove the skillet from the heat and sprinkle the cognac over the livers. Ignite with a lighted match; then shake the pan back and forth for several seconds until the flames subside. Return the pan to the heat. Add the remaining 4 tablespoons of butter, salt, pepper, and tarragon. Stir over low heat until the butter is melted.

78

While hot, turn the contents of the skillet into a blender container. Add the cream and blend until very smooth. (A food processor may be used; if small capacity, blend half the livers and half the cream at one time, then fold together.)

Pour into a large, shallow glass bowl or compote (preferably). Shake lightly to level; then let stand at room temperature until set.

Spoon the Aspic Glaze over the top, using just enough to make a thin covering. Let stand in a cool place until the aspic has set. (The pâté will improve in flavor if left to age for 24 hours.)

When ready to serve, prepare the Tomato Rose Garnish and arrange on the aspic as directed. Serve as a spread with the Toasted French Bread Slices.

Makes about 4 cups.

ASPIC GLAZE

Sprinkle 1 package of unflavored gelatin over ¼ cup cold water; let stand 5 minutes. Add ½ cup hot water (from the tap) and stir until the gelatin is dissolved. Then stir in ¼ cup cold water. Use immediately before it begins to set.

TOMATO ROSE GARNISH

Using a thin, sharp knife, peel the skin from a tomato in a continuous spiral strip about ½-inch wide. Start at the base of the tomato (not the blossom end) and keep the strip thin and with as little flesh as possible. (The strip will break into sections.) Take the longest strip and coil into a loose scroll, the skin on the outside. Take a second strip, and form into a tight scroll. Insert in the middle of the first one to form a center. With fingers, carefully transfer the tomato rose to one side of the dish. Repeat the process to make a smaller rose, using another tomato if necessary. Use the thin peeling of a cucumber or scallion top for the stems and leaves (cut with scissors). Your own decorative ability will guide you here.

Note: Although appearing to be complicated, this garnish is easily prepared—nearly always with professional results.

TOASTED FRENCH BREAD SLICES

Cut a long thin loaf (1½ inches in diameter) into ¼-inch slices. Place on a baking sheet and toast in a broiler on one side until golden; turn and toast the other side. Set aside until cool. They should be dry and crisp.

ꞭOT ꞭORS D'OEUVRES

These hot appetizers include deep-fried Artichoke Fritters served with a warm, Greek lemon sauce; unusual Eggplant Puffs; and tiny Fried Olives in Cheese Jackets. There are familiar Quiche Lorraine and a little known cheddar cheese pie called Gâteau Fromage. There are savory hot spreads, best represented by Baked Crabmeat Spread with a garnish of toasted almonds; Egg and Anchovy Turnovers made with a high rising cream cheese pastry; and toasted Hot Shrimp Canapés, as pretty and as easily made an hors d'oeuvre as you may ever come across.

RUMAKI

This is a mini version of the popular bacon-wrapped chicken liver and water chestnut hors d'oeuvre.

- 1 **can (8 ounces) water chestnuts**
- 2 **tablespoons soy sauce**
- ½ **pound chicken livers**
- 2 **tablespoons peanut or vegetable oil**
- 1 **pound thin-sliced bacon (22 to 24 slices), at room temperature**

Drain the water chestnuts; cut into fourths (or sixths if large). Place in a small bowl; add the soy sauce, turning to coat. Set aside to marinate while preparing the chicken livers.

Sauté the chicken livers in the oil over medium-high heat, turning occasionally, until they are cooked through, but still pink in the centers. This will take about 7 minutes. (Do not overcook.) Remove from heat and cool.

When cool enough to handle, cut the livers in small pieces the same size as the chestnuts. Drain the water chestnuts. Cut the bacon into thirds (easiest if cut before separating). Wrap a strip of bacon around one piece of chicken liver and one piece of water chestnut. Secure with a toothpick. As the rumaki are assembled, place them in ungreased pie plates (you will need 4 pie plates for this amount).

When ready to serve, bake one plate at a time to insure that they will be served piping hot. Bake in a preheated 500° oven 5 minutes, or until the bacon is crisp. Drain on paper toweling, then serve immediately.
Makes 5 to 6 dozen rumaki.

FRENCH FRIED MUSHROOMS
WITH TARTAR SAUCE

A perfectly delicious hors d'oeuvre, which may be prepared partially in advance, but must be fried at the last minute.

1 pound medium-size (1- to 1½-inch) fresh
   mushrooms (firm and with no gills showing)

2 eggs

4 tablespoons olive oil

1 teaspoon salt

   Flour

   Fine, dry bread crumbs

   Oil, for deep frying

   Tartar Sauce (recipe follows)

Trim the stem ends of the mushrooms, leaving the stems attached. Wipe the mushrooms clean with damp paper toweling.

Beat the eggs in a small bowl with the olive oil and salt, just enough to blend.

Roll the mushrooms in the flour, then in the egg mixture, then coat with the bread crumbs. (At this point, the mushrooms can be stored in the refrigerator until needed.)

Pour enough oil in a large heavy saucepan or deep fat fryer to reach a depth of 3 inches. Heat to 375°.

Drop the mushrooms into the oil, several at a time. (Group them according to size.) Fry, turning, until golden brown, a minute or less. Then transfer with a slotted spoon

83

to paper towels for draining. Serve immediately with Tartar Sauce and cocktail picks for dipping.
Makes 24 to 30, depending on size.

TARTAR SAUCE

1 teaspoon onion, finely chopped

2 teaspoons sweet pickles, finely chopped

1 teaspoon pimiento-stuffed olives, finely chopped and well drained

1½ teaspoons capers, finely chopped and well drained

1 tablespoon parsley, finely chopped

¾ cup mayonnaise

1 tablespoon tarragon vinegar

1 teaspoon light cream

Fold the onion, pickles, olives, capers, and parsley into the mayonnaise. Blend in the vinegar and cream. Refrigerate and serve chilled. (May be made several days in advance.)
Makes 1 cup.

ARTICHOKE FRITTERS WITH AVGOLÉMONO SAUCE

Delicious crisp morsels served with a creamy Greek lemon sauce. The fritters and sauce may be prepared in advance and reheated.

1 can (14 ounces) artichoke hearts in brine (6 to 8 hearts)

¾ cup beer

½ cup sifted all-purpose flour

1½ teaspoons salt

1 teaspoon paprika

Flour, for coating

Oil, for deep frying

Avgolémono Sauce (recipe follows)

Drain the artichoke hearts and rinse with cold water. Squeeze out the excess moisture with your fingers, then cut in quarters. Place between double thicknesses of paper toweling and press out the remaining moisture. (This is important; if moist, the fritters will be soggy.)

Combine the beer, the ½ cup flour, salt, and paprika in a small mixing bowl. Beat with a wire whisk until thoroughly blended.

Pour enough oil in a large heavy saucepan or deep fryer to reach a depth of 3 inches. Heat to 375°.

Dredge a few artichoke pieces at a time in flour; shake off excess. One by one, spear each piece with a fork; dip into the batter, drain off excess and push with your finger into the hot oil. Fry until golden brown and crisp, turning to fry evenly. Remove with a slotted spoon and drain on paper toweling. Repeat the process with the remaining artichokes. (You should be able to do at least a third of the artichokes at one time.)

Serve hot with cocktail picks and warm Avgolémono Sauce for dipping.

Makes 24 to 32 fritters.

Note: The fritters may be fried in advance and reheated on a baking sheet in a 375° oven just before serving.

AVGOLÉMONO SAUCE

> **2 teaspoons cornstarch**
>
> **1 tablespoon lemon juice**
>
> **2 egg yolks**
>
> **½ teaspoon salt**
>
> **Dash of cayenne pepper**
>
> **1 cup chicken broth**

Dissolve the cornstarch in the lemon juice in a small heavy saucepan. Add the egg yolks, salt, and cayenne pepper. Stir with a wire whisk to blend, then stir in the chicken broth.

Cook over medium heat, stirring constantly, until the mixture begins to thicken and coats a spoon (it should not approach a boil). Remove from heat and serve immediately, or set over hot water to keep warm until ready to serve. (If preferred, cool, then cover and refrigerate. Reheat slowly, stirring until warm.)

Makes about 1¼ cups.

EGGPLANT PUFFS

Crispy outside, tender within. Cheddar cheese and eggplant make a memorable combination.

1 medium eggplant (about 1 pound)

¾ cup cheddar cheese, grated

1 egg, slightly beaten

¾ teaspoon garlic salt

¾ cup Italian flavored bread crumbs

2 teaspoons lemon juice

Flour, for coating

Olive oil, for shallow frying

Peel the eggplant; cut into 1-inch cubes. Place in a sauce-pan and cover with water; bring to a boil, then simmer until tender, about 12 minutes. Drain the eggplant cubes in a colander; press with a spoon to squeeze out most of the juice; then press between folds of paper toweling to extract the remaining moisture. The eggplant cubes must be dry. While hot, mash with a fork, or use a food processor.

Stir the cheese into the warm eggplant (it should melt slightly). Add the egg, garlic salt, bread crumbs, and lemon juice. Mix well.

Scoop up about a teaspoonful of the mixture and form into a ball; place on a cookie sheet. Repeat with the remaining mixture (the balls may be placed close together). Re-frigerate until cold and firm, about 2 hours.

When ready to serve, coat with flour.

Heat enough oil in a skillet to come up the sides at least 1 inch. (Choose a medium-size skillet, so as not to waste

87

the oil.) When the oil is very hot, slide in as many of balls as will fit without crowding. Fry until golden brown, then transfer to paper towels to drain. Continue with the remainder. (The oil may be strained through a thickness of paper towel and reused for sautéing.)

Serve warm.

Makes about 36 puffs.

Note: The puffs may be fried in advance and frozen. Reheat (frozen) in a 375° oven for about 20 minutes.

GLAZED COCKTAIL FRANKS

This is a last minute hors d'oeuvre that takes only minutes to do.

1 package (5 ounces) smoked cocktail franks

2 tablespoons butter

2 tablespoons dry mustard

2 tablespoons dry sherry

Cut the cocktail franks across into halves. There are 16 in a package; you will have 32.

Melt the butter over low heat in a medium-size heavy skillet. Dissolve the dry mustard in the sherry; blend into the butter.

Add the cocktail franks; sauté slowly, turning occasionally, until the moisture has evaporated and the franks are glazed. This takes only a few minutes.

Serve hot with toothpicks for spearing.

Makes 32.

SWEDISH HAM BALLS

Glazed with a sweet and sour sauce and served from a chafing dish.

1 pound smoked ham, ground

1½ pounds ground lean pork

4 cups fresh bread crumbs

2 eggs

1 cup milk

1½ cups dark brown sugar (packed)

1 teaspoon dry mustard

½ cup cider vinegar

½ cup water

Combine the ham, pork, bread crumbs, eggs, and milk; mix well. Shape into small balls, about 1 inch in diameter. Place close together in a large jelly roll pan in one layer. Chill 1 hour.

Combine the brown sugar and dry mustard in a saucepan. Add the vinegar and water. Heat, stirring, just long enough to dissolve the sugar. Pour over the chilled ham balls.

Bake uncovered in a preheated 350° oven for 45 to 50 minutes, or until well browned and glazed. (Baste and turn occasionally while baking.)

Transfer the glazed ham balls to a chafing dish or serving casserole placed over a heating device. Have toothpicks available.

Makes about 100 ham balls.

Note: *These ham balls should be baked and served at once. They will harden and lose their glaze if baked in advance, then reheated.*

DEVILED CLAM DIP

A spicy dip served from a chafing dish, to be spooned onto small slices of toasted French bread.

1 cup onions, finely chopped

6 tablespoons butter

2 cans (6 ounces each) minced clams, well drained

½ cup chili sauce

2 tablespoons Worcestershire sauce

2 tablespoons sherry (any type)

Toasted French Bread Slices (see page 80)

Sauté the onions in the butter until limp (do not brown). Stir in the clams, chili sauce, Worcestershire sauce, and sherry. Cook, stirring, for a few minutes until the sauce thickens slightly. Refrigerate several hours or overnight to blend the flavors.

Reheat before serving in a chafing dish, or a suitable serving container set over a warmer. Serve with Toasted French Bread Slices.

Makes about 2¾ cups.

HOT BLACK BEAN DIP

A heavy-handed dip from the Tex-Mex kitchens. Substantial and good.

>   2   tablespoons butter
>
>   1   large onion, grated
>
>   1   can (10½ ounces) condensed black bean soup
>
>   ¼   cup water
>
>   3   cloves garlic, finely chopped
>
>   1   tablespoon chili powder
>
>   ¼   teaspoon Tabasco sauce
>
>   ½   teaspoon salt
>
>   ½   pound longhorn (colby) cheese, grated
>
>   Tortilla chips (not flavored)

Melt the butter in a heavy saucepan over low heat. Add the onion; sauté until soft.

Add the black bean soup, water, garlic, chili powder, Tabasco, and salt; blend until smooth. Simmer uncovered for 20 minutes, stirring occasionally. Remove from the heat.

Add the grated cheese; stir until melted. Cover and let stand several hours (or refrigerate overnight) to blend the flavors.

When ready to serve, reheat slowly. Add a little water if necessary to thin to consistency for dipping. Turn into a chafing dish or a serving container set over a candle to keep warm. Serve with tortilla chips for dipping.

Makes 3½ cups.

Note: If left standing for any length of time, a thin crust will form on top; frequent dipping will eliminate the problem.

HOT CAMEMBERT DIP

A good way to stretch expensive Camembert cheese. The mixture tastes buttery and is enough for a crowd.

2 packages (4 ounces each) Camembert
2 packages (8 ounces each) cream cheese
   Paprika and finely chopped parsley, for garnish
   Assorted crackers

Scrape the coating (rind) from the Camembert cheese, using a small sharp knife. Cut the cheese into chunks and place in the top of a double boiler. Add the cream cheese, cut similarly. Set over boiling water. Heat, stirring occasionally, until the cheese is melted, and the two are blended completely.

Turn into a chafing dish or a heated serving bowl. Sprinkle the top lightly with paprika and a few flakes of parsley for color. Include an assortment of crackers and a knife for spreading.

Makes 6 cups.

Note: In a chafing dish, the mixture will keep well for dipping throughout serving. In a heated bowl, it will hold for at least 30 minutes. Even as it cools, the consistency will still be spreadable, as both are soft cheeses.

BAKED CRABMEAT SPREAD

A rich, hot spread to delight all crab lovers.

> 1 package (8 ounces) cream cheese, at room
> temperature
> 1 tablespoon milk
> 2 teaspoons Worcestershire sauce
> 1 package (6 ounces) frozen crabmeat, thawed
> 2 tablespoons chives or scallion tops, chopped
> ⅓ cup slivered toasted almonds
> Assorted crackers

Blend the cream cheese with the milk and Worcestershire sauce.

Drain the crabmeat. Pick over for any cartilage, then shred the meat coarsely with your fingers. Add to the cream-cheese mixture along with the chives; mix lightly.

Turn into a greased, 8-inch shallow casserole or pie plate. Sprinkle the almonds over the top. (May be prepared in advance to this point.)

When ready to serve, bake in a preheated 350° oven until heated through and bubbling, about 15 minutes. Keep the cocktail spread warm over a candle warmer. Serve with assorted crackers.

Makes about 2½ cups.

GÂTEAU FROMAGE

A golden-topped cheddar cheese pie. Beautiful to look at, easy to make, and delicious to eat.

An 8-inch unbaked pastry shell (recipe follows)

1/2 **pound sharp cheddar cheese, grated (2 cups)**

1 **egg, beaten until foamy**

1 **tablespoon flour**

1 **cup (scant) milk**

Prepare the pastry shell as directed. Press the edges with the tines of a fork instead of fluting. (A high edge will burn.) Do not prick the pastry before baking.

Sprinkle the cheese loosely into the bottom of the pastry shell. (May be prepared in advance to this point.)

Combine the beaten egg, flour, and milk. (A few seconds in a blender or food processor will simplify the procedure—the egg need not be beaten in advance.) Pour the mixture over the cheese; do not stir—simply jiggle the plate to settle the mixture.

Bake in a preheated 450° oven for 20 to 25 minutes, or until a knife inserted in the center comes out clean. Let stand a few minutes, or until the pie can be cut neatly, but is still hot.

Cut into 6 or 8 wedges. You will need small plates and forks.

Makes 6 to 8 servings.

PASTRY

1 **cup plus 2 tablespoons sifted all-purpose flour**

1/2 **teaspoon salt**

6 **tablespoons vegetable shortening**

2 1/2 **to 3 tablespoons cold water**

Sift the flour and salt together into a mixing bowl. Cut in half of the shortening with a pastry blender until it looks like coarse meal. Cut in the remainder of the shortening until it is the size of large peas.

Sprinkle the cold water over the mixture, a tablespoon at a time. Mix lightly with a fork until all the flour is moistened and the dough barely clings together.

Roll the dough out on a lightly floured board to a ⅛-inch thickness. Transfer to an 8-inch pie plate; trim the edges to a ½-inch overhang; then fold under and press the edges with the tines of a fork.

Note: This amount of pastry is also suitable for a 9-inch shell.

QUICHE LORRAINE

There are many recipes for this classic French tart; this is my favorite.

A 9-inch unbaked pastry shell (see page 95)

4 **thin strips bacon**

1 **cup Gruyère cheese, coarsely grated**

3 **eggs**

1½ **cups light cream**

½ **teaspoon salt**

¼ **teaspoon white pepper**

¼ **teaspoon (scant) nutmeg, freshly grated**

Line a 9-inch pie plate with pastry. Flute the edges with the fingers. (Do not prick.) Bake in a preheated 450° oven for 5 minutes. If pastry puffs, as it cools press back into shape with fingertips. Cool.

Fry the bacon until crisp. Drain on paper toweling. Crumble and sprinkle over the bottom of the pie shell. Sprinkle the cheese loosely over the bacon. (May be prepared in advance to this point.)

Beat the eggs with the cream, salt, white pepper, and nutmeg, just until blended. Use a wire whisk, or put into a blender for a few seconds. Pour over the cheese.

Bake in a preheated 450° oven for 15 minutes; then reduce the heat to 350° and bake until a knife inserted 1 inch from the pastry edge comes out clean, about 10 minutes longer. Cool a few minutes until it can be cut neatly and serve warm. Cut into 8 to 10 wedges. You will need small plates and forks.

Makes 8 to 10 servings.

EGG AND ANCHOVY TURNOVERS

Rich flaky pastry with a savory filling. This is a two-in-one recipe. The pastry scraps are rolled, cut, and topped with poppy or sesame seeds to make miniature biscuits.

> 2　cups unsifted all-purpose flour
>
> ½　teaspoon salt
>
> ½　pound (2 sticks) butter, at room temperature
>
> 2　packages (3 ounces each) cream cheese, at room temperature
>
> 　　Egg and Anchovy Filling (recipe follows)
>
> 1　egg beaten slightly with 1 teaspoon water (glaze)
>
> 　　Poppy seeds or sesame seeds

Combine the flour and salt in a mixing bowl. Cut in the butter and cream cheese, using a pastry blender at first. Then knead with your hand just until blended and the dough clings together and leaves the sides of the bowl. Form into a ball. If too soft for rolling, chill briefly.

Roll out half the dough at a time between two sheets of waxed paper to slightly less than ⅛-inch thickness. Cut into rounds with a 3-inch cookie cutter.

Place about a teaspoon of filling in the center of each round. Using your finger, brush the edges of the pastry with the beaten egg. Fold in half and seal the edges by pressing together; then press again with the tines of a fork. Make a small hole in the center of each with a toothpick to allow the steam to escape. Then brush the tops of the pastries with the egg glaze. (The pastries may be made in advance to this point and refrigerated several hours or overnight.)

Place an inch apart on an ungreased baking sheet. Bake in a preheated 400° oven for 12 minutes (15 if chilled), or until golden on top and well browned on the bottom. Serve hot. *Makes 24.*

Note: Press the scraps of dough together and reroll slightly more than ⅛-inch thick. Cut into rounds with a 1¼-inch cutter. Brush the tops with egg, and sprinkle with poppy seeds or sesame seeds. Bake at 400° for about 10 minutes. (They will triple in size; you should have about 3 dozen biscuits.) Once served, they may be split and filled with a dab of any spread you might be serving.

EGG AND ANCHOVY FILLING

2 large hard-cooked eggs

1 can (2 ounces) anchovies

2 tablespoons soft butter

3 tablespoons parsley, finely chopped

2 tablespoons (scant) onion, finely chopped

Slice the eggs into a mixing bowl; chop fine with a pastry blender. Drain the anchovies, reserving the oil, and chop fine on a cutting board. Add to the eggs along with the butter, parsley, and onion. Mix together with a fork, adding just enough of the anchovy oil to bind (about 2 teaspoons).

HOT SHRIMP CANAPÉS

Toasted treasures with the prize right on top. As beautiful to look at as they are delicious to eat.

1 can (4¼ ounces) small shrimp (see note)
15 to 18 slices white sandwich bread (1 pound loaf)
¾ cup mayonnaise
6 tablespoons Parmesan cheese, grated
1 tablespoon scallion tops, finely chopped

Drain the shrimp; rinse with cold water and drain again.

Cut the bread into rounds using a 1½-inch cutter. (You should be able to cut four rounds from each slice to make 60 to 72 rounds.)

Combine the mayonnaise, Parmesan cheese, and scallion tops. Using a table knife, place a dollop of the mixture (about ½ teaspoon) in the center of each bread round. Do not spread to the edges. Press one shrimp lightly into the center.

Place on a baking sheet and broil about 4 inches from the source of heat about 2 minutes, or until the cheese is bubbly and the edges of the bread are toasted. Serve hot.

The canapés may be prepared up to broiling, covered, and refrigerated several hours in advance. Aluminum pie plates are good storage containers; a 9-inch plate holds 16.

Makes 5 to 6 dozen canapés.

Note: Small shrimp, not tiny ones, are required. There are about 60 to 70 shrimp in one can, depending on brand. Cut an equal number of bread rounds.

HOT CURRIED CHEESE CANAPÉS

Attractive broiled canapés. The curry powder is light but influential. A slice of black olive in the center of the golden filling lends a color accent.

½ cup sharp cheddar cheese, grated

½ cup (scant) mayonnaise

2 tablespoons scallions, finely chopped (including tops)

¼ teaspoon salt

¼ teaspoon (scant) curry powder

9 slices white sandwich bread

Black olives (see note)

Using a fork, mash the cheese with the mayonnaise until fairly smooth. Stir in the scallions, salt, and curry powder.

Cut the bread into rounds, using a 1½-inch cutter. You will need about 36 bread rounds.

Using a table knife, place a dollop of the cheese mixture (about 1 teaspoon) in the center of each bread round. Do not spread to the edges.

Cut thin, lengthwise slices from the olives; use to garnish the centers of the canapés. (May be prepared ahead to this point; cover and refrigerate.)

Place on a baking sheet and broil about 4 inches from the source of heat, for about 2 minutes, or until the cheese is bubbly and the edges of the bread are toasted. Serve hot.

Makes about 3 dozen canapés.

Note: Select-size ripe olives with pits are small enough to produce attractive ovals when sliced.

TOASTED CHEESE ON RYE

An easy recipe for an informal occasion.

32 to 36 slices party rye bread (1 loaf)

1 cup sharp cheddar cheese, grated

2 tablespoons mayonnaise

1 tablespoon milk

6 tablespoons onion, chopped (not fine)

¼ teaspoon garlic salt

Toast the bread slices on one side only on a baking sheet placed in a preheated broiler. Remove from the oven, but leave the bread on the baking sheet.

Combine the cheese, mayonnaise, milk, onion, and garlic salt in a small, heavy skillet. Set over direct, low heat, stirring until the cheese is melted. Use at once.

One by one, turn the bread slices and spread the untoasted sides (to the edges) with the cheese mixture; replace on the baking sheet. (If the cheese cools, reheat just until spreadable.)

These may be prepared several hours in advance; cover with plastic wrap and let stand at room temperature. If held longer, refrigerate.

To serve, broil until the cheese bubbles lightly. Serve hot. Depending on number of guests, you may want to broil in several batches. They cool quickly.

Makes about 3 dozen canapés.

OLIVES IN CHEESE JACKETS

Delicious tidbits made with pimiento-stuffed olives. They are easily prepared, but require last minute deep frying.

28 to 32 whole pimiento-stuffed olives (the smallest available)

2 egg whites (from large eggs)

1 cup Jarlsberg cheese, grated (see note)

Fine dry bread crumbs

Oil, for deep frying

Drain the olives, then dry on paper toweling.

Beat the egg whites until soft peaks form; fold in the cheese. Using your fingers, press about a teaspoon of the mixture around an olive, as best you can. (It need not cover evenly at this point.) Then roll with fingertips in the palm of your other hand to firm and even out the coating.

Roll in the bread crumbs; then roll again between the palms of your hands so that the crumbs adhere firmly. (The process may seem difficult, but it is not.) At this point the olives may be stored in the refrigerator until needed, but they should be chilled at least 1 hour.

Pour enough oil in a skillet to cover the olives well. Heat to 350°.

Fry the olives, about one third at a time, in the hot oil until golden brown, about 1 minute. Drain on paper towels. Serve hot. This is finger food; picks are not necessary.

Makes 28 to 32.

Note: Jarlsberg cheese is a semisoft Swiss type cheese.

GOUGÈRES

These savory cheese puffs are miniature versions of the famous Burgundian pastry. They can be made in advance and reheated.

½ cup water

4 tablespoons butter, in slices

½ teaspoon (scant) salt

½ cup sifted all-purpose flour

2 large eggs

1½ teaspoons Dijon mustard

¼ cup Swiss cheese, finely grated

¼ cup Parmesan cheese, finely grated

1 egg yolk, slightly beaten with 1 teaspoon water

Combine the water, butter, and salt in a small, heavy saucepan; bring to a rolling boil over medium heat. Add the flour all at once; turn the heat to low and beat briskly with a wooden spoon until the mixture leaves the sides of the pan.

Remove from the heat and beat in the eggs, one at a time. (Do not add the second egg until the first has been completely incorporated.)

Stir in the mustard, Swiss cheese, and Parmesan cheese. Cool slightly for easier handling.

Drop by slightly rounded measuring teaspoonfuls onto a greased baking sheet, about an inch apart. Brush the tops lightly with the beaten egg yolk, smoothing them lightly. (Your finger works best here.) You will need two sheets; bake them one at a time.

Bake in a preheated 450° oven for 5 minutes; reduce heat

to 400° and bake 15 to 18 minutes longer until puffed and golden brown. They should feel crisp and dry. Serve warm. *Makes about 48 small puffs.*

Note: These may be baked in advance and cooled on the baking sheet, then reheated briefly in a 350° oven.

CHEESE BISCUITS

Golden pastry wafers—just right for two bites.

½ **cup (1 stick) butter, softened**

½ **pound sharp cheddar cheese, grated (2 cups)**

1 **cup sifted all-purpose flour**

Dash of cayenne pepper

Paprika

Work the butter, cheese, flour, and cayenne pepper together with your hands until well blended. Form into ¾-inch balls. Chill for at least 1 hour.

Place 1½ inches apart on an ungreased cookie sheet. Bake in a preheated 400° oven until golden, about 15 minutes. Sprinkle lightly with paprika after removing from the oven. Serve warm.

Makes about 4 dozen wafers.

Note: The dough may be formed into balls and placed close together in a baking pan, covered tightly, and kept refrigerated up to two weeks. The dough is then handy for baking a few biscuits at a time.

COLD BUFFET DISHES

An array of festive dishes is included here: main dishes, salads, marinated vegetables, and relishes. Buffet spectaculars featured are golden roasted Smoked Turkey; Cold Roast Fillet of Beef; Glazed Cold Ham with a warm Creamy Mustard Sauce; Daube Glacé, a New Orleans jellied beef mold; Jambon Persillé, a mold of cubed ham with a thick layer of parsley aspic on top; and well-seasoned Country Pâté. Among the accompaniments are Holiday Cheese, made with cottage cheese and a dozen flavoring ingredients; an unusual chopped Russian Potato Salad containing salami; a chef's salad called Grandfather's Salad; Seafoam Salad made with pears; and Marinated Artichoke Hearts, a facsimile of the purchased variety.

SMOKED TURKEY

Nothing enhances a holiday buffet like cold smoked turkey. This version is easy to prepare—thanks to liquid smoke—and produced at one-third the cost of its mail-order counterpart.

An 18- to 22-pound fresh or frozen turkey

Salt

5 or 6 cloves garlic

Liquid smoke (see note)

1 cup water

1 bay leaf, crumbled

1 tablespoon mustard seed

6 peppercorns

¼ pound (1 stick) butter

Thaw the turkey if frozen, according to packer's directions. Remove the giblets (they are not used here). Rinse, then dry the turkey thoroughly.

Rub the skin and the cavity of the turkey well with salt, then rub again with a cut clove of garlic or two. Place 2 cloves of garlic in the cavity.

With the tip of a knife, make a slit in the skin and flesh on each side of the thickest part of the breast; insert a clove of garlic in each.

Using a pastry brush, paint the turkey (skin and cavity) with liquid smoke. Wrap securely with foil, then refrigerate overnight.

The next morning, remove the turkey from the refrigerator and let stand (wrapped) until it reaches room temperature. This will take several hours.

Unwrap the turkey, set on a metal rack, and place in a large roasting pan. Combine the water, 1 tablespoon liquid smoke, bay leaf, mustard seed, and peppercorns; pour into the sides of the pan. Place into a preheated 325° oven; roast for 20 minutes.

Rub the turkey skin with the stick of butter. (For convenience, leave the butter in its wrapping and apply directly.) Then baste with the liquid from the pan. Repeat this procedure several times throughout the roasting, basting first, then rubbing the bird with butter. Continue roasting until the turkey is cooked through, from 4 to 6 hours.

Note: There are several tests for doneness: a thermometer inserted in the thickest part of the breast should register 175°; the leg (at its joint with the thigh) should move easily up and down; or the fleshiest part of the leg should feel soft. All of these are more accurate than mere timing, since the age, weight, and temperature of the bird, plus the cooling off of the oven when opened (for basting) will alter exact timing.

Remove from the oven and allow to cool to room temperature. Wrap, then refrigerate overnight, but remove long enough in advance so that the turkey may be served close to room temperature.

Makes 20 or more servings, with leftovers.

Note: This process takes 3 days: the turkey is painted with the liquid smoke one day, baked the second, and then served the third day.

For an attractive presentation, carve half of the bird (one side) into thin slices. Place the carved turkey on a large serving platter; then arrange the slices, overlapping, around it. Place a large bunch of parsley along the cut side as camouflage. Carve additional slices as needed.

Liquid smoke is a commercial product. It may be purchased in retail markets that specialize in gourmet foods.

COLD CHICKEN IN ASPIC

A molded delight that elevates cold chicken to the status of important buffet fare.

A 3½- to 3¾-pound chicken, cut up

3 cups water

1 small onion, sliced

2 celery tops

2 bay leaves

2 teaspoons salt

2 envelopes unflavored gelatin

¼ cup cold water

3 hard-cooked eggs

½ cup pecans, coarsely broken

Ripe olives, for garnish

Watercress sprigs, for garnish

Place the chicken pieces in a heavy saucepan. Add the water, onion, celery tops, bay leaves, and salt. Bring to a boil; cover and reduce the heat. Simmer 35 to 40 minutes, or until tender. Remove the chicken and cool until it can be handled. Pull the chicken from the bones in large pieces, discarding the skin. Cut into fairly thick slices.

Strain the broth and skim off all the fat. Measure 2¾ cups; set aside.

Soften the gelatin in the ¼ cup cold water in a saucepan. Add the chicken broth; heat, stirring until the gelatin is dissolved.

Pour a thin layer of the broth into a 9 × 5 × 3-inch loaf

pan, which has been rinsed with cold water; let stand until cool. Cut one of the eggs in half lengthwise and place end-to-end, cut side down, in the center of the pan. Chill until firm.

Allow the remaining broth to cool until it begins to thicken, then add the chicken and pecans. Spoon over the eggs and aspic. Refrigerate until firm. (May be kept several days before serving.)

When ready to serve, unmold the chicken onto a serving tray or cutting board. Cut the remaining 2 eggs into lengthwise quarters, and arrange around the sides along with the olives and sprigs of watercress. Cut into slices when serving.
Makes 8 or more servings.

Note: Mayonnaise and crisp salted crackers or potato chips are good accompaniments.

CHICKEN TROPICALE

A chicken salad that combines the chicken with pineapple cubes, grapes, celery, and almonds presented attractively in fresh pineapple shells.

2 small fresh pineapples, with attractive fronds

1 large seedless orange

½ cup green grapes, halved

½ cup celery (from inner stalks), diced

4 cups cooked chicken, cut into bite-size cubes

¾ cup toasted slivered almonds

1 teaspoon salt

½ teaspoon crushed dried mint

¾ cup mayonnaise

1 cup heavy cream, whipped

Cut the pineapples in half lengthwise, including the fronds. With a small sharp knife, score the flesh around the rim ½ inch inside the skin. Then cut along both sides of the core at an angle; pull out and discard. Make a second verticle incision in the cavity left to within ½ inch of the bottom (to aid in releasing the flesh.) Then carefully cut from the bottom and remove the flesh, leaving the shell ½ inch thick. Cut the flesh into bite-size pieces.

Peel the orange, trimming away all the spongy white part. Hold the orange over a small bowl; cut on either side of the membrane to release the sections. Squeeze the pulp to extract the juice, reserving 2 tablespoons. Cut the orange sec-

112

tions into bite-size pieces. Combine with the pineapple, grapes, celery, chicken, and ¼ cup of the almonds.

Blend the reserved orange juice, salt, and mint into the mayonnaise; fold in the whipped cream. Lightly mix with the combined fruit mixture; pile into the pineapple shells. Sprinkle the remaining almonds on top and chill until ready to serve. (For best flavor, it should not be icy cold.)

Makes 6 or more servings.

Note: For an attractive presentation, arrange the pineapple halves on a large platter (in a cross) with fronds extending over the edge. Arrange clusters of sugared, fresh green grapes between the shells. To prepare, pull off small clusters of grapes (stems attached) from a bunch of grapes. Dip them in egg whites, beaten only enough to liquefy, but not foamy, then dip into granulated sugar. Set on a rack to dry.

SHRIMP IN LETTUCE CUPS

Shrimp for guests suggest you really care.

2 pounds medium-size shrimp in the shell, cooked
(see method below)

2 egg yolks

1 teaspoon Dijon mustard

6 tablespoons olive oil

2 tablespoons tarragon vinegar

1 tablespoon lemon juice

1 clove garlic, finely chopped

Salt, to taste

Cayenne pepper, to taste

6 hard-cooked eggs, coarsely chopped

16 leaves Boston lettuce

16 cherry tomatoes

16 black olives

Peel and devein the shrimp; set aside.

In a large mixing bowl, whip the egg yolks with the mustard, oil, and vinegar. Blend in the lemon juice, garlic, salt, and cayenne pepper to taste. Add the shrimp and hard-cooked eggs; mix well. Chill at least 1 hour.

Arrange two lettuce leaves (cupped) on each of 8 plates. Spoon equal portions of the shrimp into the lettuce cups. Garnish each with cherry tomatoes and olives.

Makes 8 servings.

Bring 2 quarts of water to a boil with 16 whole cloves, 4 tablespoons vinegar, 4 pods dried red peppers, and 2 tablespoons salt; simmer 5 minutes. Add the shrimp, and cook gently about 10 minutes, or until cooked through. Remove with a slotted spoon and cool.

GLAZED COLD HAM WITH CREAMY MUSTARD SAUCE

Canned ham with a spruced-up presentation. The ham is glazed with a wine-flavored aspic, the sides coated with chopped parsley, and then it is displayed on a platter surrounded by chopped aspic, which shines like jewels. The accompanying sauce is so good, you may be tempted to eat it with a spoon.

> **A 5-pound canned ham, chilled**
>
> 1 **envelope unflavored gelatin**
>
> 2 **tablespoons cold water**
>
> 1 **can (10½ ounces) beef consommé**
>
> ¼ **cup port or Madeira wine**
>
> **Chopped parsley**
>
> **Creamy Mustard Sauce (recipe follows)**

Remove the ham from the can. Pull off as much gelatin as you can with your fingers (it is not needed here). Place the ham under running hot tap water to dissolve the remainder. Dry thoroughly on paper toweling. Set on a rack over a pan.

Sprinkle the gelatin over the 2 tablespoons cold water in a small saucepan. When softened, add ¼ cup of the consommé (do not dilute). Cook, stirring, over low heat until the gelatin is dissolved. Remove from the heat and stir in the remaining consommé, then the wine. Let stand until syrupy.

Pour a little of the syrupy gelatin mixture over the top of the ham, allowing the excess to drip down the sides. Quickly spread the sides with a knife or pastry brush so that all parts are coated. (The sides will barely be coated, but the top should have a thin glaze; add a little more gelatin mixture to the top if necessary.) If an excess of the glaze has dripped off, return it to the saucepan.

Before the glaze sets on the sides of the ham, press the chopped parsley into it. (The parsley need not cover evenly, but use enough so that the sides are attractively garnished.) Chill until ready to serve.

Pour the remaining gelatin mixture (aspic) into an 8-inch-square pan. Let stand, or chill until set. (If it has started to jell, reheat to liquefy.)

When ready to serve, place the ham on a large serving platter. Using a table knife, score the firm aspic into tiny squares or diamonds. Loosen with a spatula and mix lightly. Spoon out, and surround the ham with these "tiny jewels." Serve chilled with warm Creamy Mustard Sauce placed in a separate bowl.

Makes 16 or more servings.

CREAMY MUSTARD SAUCE

> ½ **cup sugar**
>
> 1½ **tablespoons all-purpose flour**
>
> 2 **tablespoons dry mustard**
>
> 1 **egg yolk**
>
> 1 **cup light cream**
>
> ½ **cup cider vinegar**
>
> ½ **teaspoon salt**

Combine the sugar, flour, and dry mustard in the top of a double boiler. Stir in the egg yolk and cream. Cook, stirring, over boiling water until well thickened.

Stir in the vinegar and salt. Continue cooking and stirring just until heated through. Serve immediately, or keep warm over hot water.

Makes about 1¾ cups sauce.

Note: The sauce may be prepared a day in advance, covered, and refrigerated. Reheat over simmering water.

JAMBON PERSILLÉ

Cold parsley ham in a jellied mold—a dish that originated in Burgundy. The ham is served from the mold; each slice will contain a layer of pink jellied ham topped with a layer of green parsley aspic.

2 pounds cooked smoked ham (in one piece)

2½ cups chicken broth

1¼ cups dry white wine

3 envelopes unflavored gelatin

¼ cup cold water

1 tablespoon tarragon vinegar

1 cup parsley, finely chopped

Dijon mustard and cornichons for accompaniments (see note)

Cut the ham in irregular ½-inch cubes. Trim off any fat. (You should have about 5 cups.)

Place the ham in a saucepan. Add the chicken broth and 1 cup of the wine; simmer covered 5 minutes. Remove the ham with a slotted spoon; cool slightly. Strain the broth through a double thickness of wet paper toweling.

Place the ham in a serving bowl, 7½ to 8 inches in diameter and at least 3½ inches deep. Be sure to rinse the bowl first with cold water. (Glass is attractive, as the ham is served from the dish.) The ham cubes should be fairly level.

Soften the gelatin in the ¼ cup cold water; then dissolve in the remaining hot broth (reheat if necessary). Cool slightly, then pour 2 cups of the gelatin mixture over the ham, reserving the remainder. Chill until firm.

Stir the remaining ¼ cup wine, vinegar, and parsley into the remaining gelatin mixture. (It should be cool enough so that the parsley does not wilt.)

When the ham is set, spoon the parsley mixture over the top, spreading evenly. Chill until firm.

When ready to serve, bring the bowl to the table. Cut into wedges. Serve with cornichons and Dijon mustard.

Makes 8 or more servings.

Note: This dish may be prepared in advance. It will keep for nearly a week.

Cornichons are tiny sour pickles imported from France. They are sold in specialty shops. Substitute sliced, large sour pickles if not available.

JELLIED HAM LOAF

An especially attractive way to include ham in the buffet line-up. The sauce will steal the show.

4 envelopes unflavored gelatin

½ cup cold water

2 cups tomato juice

2 tablespoons onion, finely grated

2 tablespoons lemon juice

4 cups cooked ham, finely ground (about 2 pounds)

1 medium-size green pepper, finely chopped

1 cup mayonnaise

Crisp fresh vegetables or parsley sprigs, for garnish

Sour Cream Sauce (recipe follows)

Sprinkle the gelatin over the cold water in a small saucepan to soften. Add 1 cup of the tomato juice; heat and stir until the gelatin is dissolved. Stir in the remaining 1 cup tomato juice, grated onion, and lemon juice. Chill until syrupy.

Stir in the ground ham and chopped green pepper; then fold in the mayonnaise.

Pour into a lightly oiled 8-cup loaf pan or mold. Cover and chill overnight.

Unmold carefully before serving and garnish the platter

with crisp fresh vegetables or parsley sprigs. Cut into slices for serving.

Serve the Sour Cream Sauce separately.

Makes 8 to 10 servings.

SOUR CREAM SAUCE

> **1 cup sour cream**
>
> **1 cup applesauce**
>
> **6 tablespoons prepared horseradish, well drained**

Combine the sour cream, applesauce, and horseradish. Chill.

COLD ROAST FILLET OF BEEF

Crusty brown around the edges and pink in the center, this sliced fillet becomes the star of the buffet board. The beef is expensive, yet so easily prepared, you may willingly dismiss the cost. It is served with a whipped cream horseradish sauce.

1 whole fillet of beef (about 6 pounds untrimmed)

3 tablespoons brandy

3 tablespoons butter

2 teaspoons coarse salt

½ teaspoon freshly ground pepper

Watercress sprigs, for garnish

Whipped Horseradish Sauce (recipe follows)

Trim the layer of fat from the meat. With a small, sharp knife, trim off the sinew, which lies beneath the fat, to prevent drawing up during roasting. You will have about 3½ pounds of trimmed meat. A butcher will trim the meat for you.

Place the tenderloin on a piece of foil; draw up the sides and pour the brandy over it. Marinate at least 1 hour, turning the meat occasionally. Remove and dry with paper toweling.

Melt the butter in a shallow roasting pan over high heat. Sear the meat quickly on all sides. Remove the pan from the heat; then sprinkle the meat with the salt and pepper.

Roast in a preheated 425° oven for 15 minutes; turn, reduce the heat to 400°, and continue roasting for 15 to 20 minutes.

A meat thermometer will register 125° for rare; 135° for

medium. Remove from the oven and allow to cool, then re-frigerate.

For serving, carve the meat into thin slices. (You should have 24 to 30 slices.) Arrange the slices, overlapping, down the center of a large platter. Garnish the sides with water-cress sprigs. Serve with Whipped Horseradish Sauce.
Makes 10 or more servings.

WHIPPED HORSERADISH SAUCE

1 cup heavy cream, lightly whipped

3 tablespoons prepared horseradish, drained

Salt, to taste

Combine the whipped cream, horseradish, and salt. Chill.

DAUBE GLACÉ

Creole beef from the kitchens of Louisiana. This jellied loaf is considered a must for Mardi Gras and again on New Year's Day in some southern households.

1   3-pound bottom round roast

1   cup plus 2 tablespoons dry red wine

2   teaspoons salt

½   teaspoon Tabasco sauce

2   sprigs parsley

2   bay leaves

1   teaspoon dried thyme

2   cloves garlic

2   large onions, sliced

2   stalks celery, cut in chunks

2   carrots, cut in chunks

3   tablespoons olive oil

3   cups water

3   envelopes unflavored gelatin

1   tablespoon wine vinegar

3   egg whites, beaten until frothy

Clusters of parsley, for garnish

2   hard-cooked eggs, sliced, for garnish

Creole Mustard Sauce (recipe follows)

Place the meat in a deep glass, stainless steel, or enamel dish. Combine 1 cup of the wine, salt, and Tabasco; pour over the meat. Add the parsley, bay leaves, thyme, garlic, onions, celery, and carrots. Cover and refrigerate overnight, turning occasionally.

Remove the meat from the marinade, reserving the marinade and vegetables.

Heat the oil in a Dutch oven or large heavy saucepan. Brown the meat on all sides. Add the reserved marinade and vegetables and 3 cups of water. Bring to a boil, then simmer slowly until tender, about 3 hours.

Remove the meat and chill until firm enough for slicing. Strain the stock and chill; remove the fat.

Measure 3½ cups of the stock into a saucepan; stir in the gelatin, wine vinegar, the remaining 2 tablespoons of wine, and the egg whites. Heat slowly until the mixture comes to a full boil. Remove from the heat and let stand 10 minutes. Strain through several thicknesses of rinsed cheesecloth, which have been placed in a sieve set over a bowl.

Note: The egg whites will collect the sediment, so that the liquid is clear.

Pour a little of the stock (aspic) into a 9 × 5 × 3-inch loaf pan, which has been rinsed in cold water; chill until firm. Let the remaining aspic stand until syrupy. Slice the meat into ⅛-inch thick slices; trim off the fat and gristle. Arrange the meat in the loaf pan, spooning a little of the syrupy aspic over each layer. Pour the remaining aspic over the top, using just enough to cover. Chill several hours, or overnight to firm.

When serving, unmold onto a platter. Garnish with parsley and the sliced eggs. Cut into thin slices and serve with the Creole Mustard Sauce.

Makes 8 or more servings.

CREOLE MUSTARD SAUCE

　　　½　cup mayonnaise

　　　½　cup sour cream

　　　1　tablespoon Creole mustard (see note)

Blend the mayonnaise, sour cream, and mustard.

　Note: Creole mustard is available in specialty stores; any grainy mustard may be substituted.

COUNTRY PÂTÉ

The king of savory pâtés. This delicious and attractive loaf is made with pork, ham, chicken livers, and spinach. Pâté lovers will nag you for the recipe.

1 pound loose spinach (or 10-ounce package)

1¼ pounds lean pork, ground

¼ pound bacon, diced

¼ pound cooked smoked ham, cut in small cubes

4 eggs, beaten slightly

1 medium onion, finely chopped

2 cloves garlic, finely chopped

2 tablespoons fresh parsley, chopped

1 teaspoon dried basil

1 teaspoon dried chervil

1 teaspoon dried rosemary

1 tablespoon salt

½ teaspoon black pepper, freshly ground

⅛ teaspoon nutmeg, freshly grated

¼ pound chicken livers

2 tablespoons butter

½ cup heavy cream

¾ to 1 pound bacon, blanched (method follows)

Remove the tough stems from the spinach. Rinse well in cold water, drain. Place in a saucepan without additional

128

water (it will cook in the water that clings to the leaves). Cover and cook 2 to 4 minutes, just until wilted, stirring once or twice. Drain in a colander; rinse with cold water and drain again. Squeeze in your hands to extract most of the remaining liquid. Chop coarsely.

Combine the pork, diced bacon, and ham. Mix in the spinach. Add the eggs, onion, garlic, parsley, basil, chervil, rosemary, salt, pepper, and nutmeg. Mix well.

Cut the chicken livers into small pieces. Sauté in the butter until stiffened, but still pink in the centers. Remove from the heat and stir in the cream. Add to the meat mixture; blend well.

Line a well buttered 9 × 5 × 3-inch loaf pan with slightly overlapping slices of the blanched bacon. To do this, lay 3 or 4 strips of the bacon lengthwise in the bottom of the pan to cover. Reserve 3 or 4 strips for the top. Cut the remaining strips into halves and arrange around the sides of the mold with the ends overhanging the top. (This is not easy, but the soft butter will help hold them in place.)

Fill the mold with the pâté mixture, mounding the top slightly. Fold the ends of the bacon over and arrange the remaining bacon lengthwise on top. Press to form a compact loaf. Cover with a double thickness of heavy foil, sealing well.

Place the loaf in a baking pan; fill with boiling water to at least 1 inch up the sides of the mold.

Bake in a preheated 350° oven for about 2 hours, or until the pâté begins to pull away from the sides of the mold and the juices are clear, not pink. (A thermometer inserted halfway in the center will register 165° to 170°.)

Remove the pâté (the mold and the baking pan) from the oven and let stand 15 minutes. Place a board on the pâté with a 3- to 4-pound weight on top. Let stand until cold. Remove the weight, then refrigerate. (The pâté will keep well for several days.)

Note: The excess liquid fat and juices will spill over the top of the mold and drip into the pan, and thus can be discarded conveniently.

For serving, unmold the pâté onto a cutting board and decorate as desired. Cut in thin slices. French bread makes a good accompaniment.

Makes 10 or more servings.

BLANCHED BACON

Place the strips (as a slab) in cold water in a saucepan; bring to a boil, then remove from the heat. Drain in a colander and dry on paper toweling. For this recipe you will need 15 or more slices (¾ to 1 pound) bacon to line the mold. The bacon used for testing was purchased in a supermarket, packaged and labelled "thin-sliced."

HOLIDAY CHEESE

A mold of cottage cheese and cream cheese, subtly flavored with a dozen seasoning ingredients. Goes well with cold smoked turkey or ham.

2½ pounds creamed cottage cheese (small curd)

1 pound cream cheese, at room temperature

3 tablespoons onion, grated

3 tablespoons lemon juice

¾ teaspoon salt

1 teaspoon Worcestershire sauce

½ teaspoon prepared mustard

⅛ teaspoon Tabasco sauce

⅛ teaspoon curry powder

½ cup plus 2 tablespoons fresh parsley, finely chopped

¾ cup pimiento-stuffed olives (salad type), well drained and chopped

3 tablespoons fine, dry bread crumbs (about)

2 tablespoons grated Parmesan cheese

3 tablespoons sour cream

Place the cottage cheese in a colander that has been lined with a double thickness of rinsed cheesecloth. Place over a bowl and let stand at least 1 hour to drain. Stir occasionally. Gather the edges of the cheesecloth and press to extract any remaining liquid.

Place the cream cheese in a large mixing bowl. Beat with a fork or an electric mixer until light. Blend in the onion, lemon juice, salt, Worcestershire sauce, mustard, Tabasco sauce, and curry powder. Gradually stir in the cottage cheese.

Add ½ cup of the parsley, olives, bread crumbs, Parmesan cheese, and sour cream; mix well. (The mixture is to be molded; if it doesn't seem firm enough, add a few more bread crumbs.)

Line an 8- to 9-cup bowl or simple mold with plastic wrap. Press the cheese mixture firmly into the mold. Place a plate on top and add a heavy weight (use a plate small enough to fit inside the mold). Refrigerate overnight.

Unmold onto a serving plate; remove the plastic wrap and sprinkle the remaining parsley over the top.

Makes 12 or more servings.

Note: The cheese mold may be made 2 or 3 days in advance; leftovers may be remolded, refrigerated, and used again.

MUSHROOM AND CHEESE SALAD

An unexpected and tasty combination.

1½ pounds fresh mushrooms (white and firm)

6 ounces thin-sliced Swiss cheese, cut in 1-inch squares

⅓ cup celery tops, chopped (mostly leaves)

⅔ cup peanut oil

¼ cup lemon juice

1¾ teaspoons salt

3 hard-cooked eggs, chopped

Cut the stems from the mushrooms at the base (the stems are not used here). Wipe the caps with damp paper towels. Cut into ⅛-inch slices.

Combine the mushrooms, cheese, and celery tops in a large salad bowl. (May be prepared in advance to this point; cover and let stand at room temperature.)

Combine the oil, lemon juice, and salt. Pour over the mushroom mixture; mix lightly (use your hands to avoid bruising). Add the chopped eggs and mix lightly again. Serve immediately.

Makes 10 or more servings.

RUSSIAN POTATO SALAD

An unusual potato salad that is especially colorful and unique in taste. It makes an excellent side dish with any meat, poultry, or fish on the buffet.

> 5 pounds potatoes (see note)
> 2 large carrots
> 1 medium-size onion
> ¼ pound hard salami
> 3 hard-cooked eggs
> 1 cup celery hearts (including leaves)
> 1½ teaspoons salt
> ¼ teaspoon pepper
> 1 cup mayonnaise

Drop the potatoes into a pot of boiling water and boil gently just until tender, about 20 minutes (do not overcook). Drain and let cool until they can be handled. Peel and cut into large chunks. Set aside.

Scrape the carrots and cut into chunks. Parboil in boiling water just until tender, about 15 minutes (so that they won't be crunchy in the salad). Set aside.

Cut the onion, salami, eggs, and celery hearts (about 1 cup celery) into chunks.

Put the potatoes, carrots, onion, salami, eggs, and celery hearts through a food chopper, using the coarse blade. (Process a little of each at a time, so that they will be partially mixed together.)

Stir the salt and pepper into the mayonnaise. Add to the

chopped ingredients; blend carefully, but well. Refrigerate
several hours to blend the flavors (overnight or longer), but
bring close to room temperature before serving.

Makes about 4 quarts.

*Note: All-purpose potatoes or boiling potatoes should be used. Baking
potatoes will break up during the chopping process.*

GRANDFATHER'S SALAD

A chef's salad that sacrifices subtlety for character. So attractive it is sure to grace any buffet.

2 heads romaine lettuce

3 heads bibb lettuce

1 cup olive oil

3 tablespoons cider vinegar

2 teaspoons salt

1 teaspoon dried tarragon

¼ teaspoon dry mustard

¼ cup parsley, finely chopped

6 hard-cooked eggs, sliced

½ pound large, fresh mushrooms (caps only), sliced

2 bunches small beets, cooked, peeled, and sliced (method follows)

2 Italian red onions, thinly sliced and separated into rings

1½ cups shredded, medium-sharp cheddar cheese

Wash the romaine and bibb lettuce; dry and tear into bite-size pieces. Chill.

Combine the oil, vinegar, salt, tarragon, and mustard. Let the dressing stand at least 30 minutes before using.

When ready to serve, toss the greens and parsley together with just enough dressing to coat lightly.

In a serving bowl, build layers of the greens with the eggs, mushrooms, beets, onions, and cheese, adding more dressing as needed.

Makes 8 to 10 servings.

TO PREPARE THE BEETS

Trim off the leaves, leaving about 2 inches of stem. Drop the beets into a saucepan of boiling water and cook for 15 to 25 minutes, or until tender. Run cold water over them just until cool enough to handle. Peel and halve lengthwise; then cut across into ⅛- to ¼-inch slices. Chill.

VIENNESE GREEN BEAN SALAD

Chilled French-cut green beans with an unusual sour cream dressing. An excellent side dish.

2 packages (10 ounces each) frozen French-cut green beans

3 egg yolks

2 tablespoons lemon juice

¼ teaspoon salt

½ cup (1 stick) sweet butter, melted and cooled

⅔ cup sour cream

Follow the package directions for thawing and cooking the green beans; drain in a colander. Then run cold water over them immediately to cool and preserve the color. Drain well; then squeeze in your hands to extract the remaining liquid. Place in a shallow serving bowl; spread out.

Place the egg yolks into the container of a blender. Add the lemon juice and salt. Blend at high speed for 2 seconds. Immediately pour in the melted butter in a slow stream of droplets. When the butter is completely added, turn off the motor. Pour into a mixing bowl. Add the sour cream; blend.

Pour the sauce into the center of the green beans; toss lightly. (The dish will be more attractive if the sauce is not mixed through completely, so that a little of the green shows.) Refrigerate (may be held overnight), but remove long enough to bring close to room temperature before serving.

Makes 8 servings.

MARINATED VEGETABLES

A perfect salad substitute—and a colorful one.

    8 cups assorted fresh vegetables (see list below)

   ¾ cup peanut oil

   ½ cup lemon juice

   ¼ cup white vinegar

   3 tablespoons sugar

   1 tablespoon salt

1½ teaspoons dried oregano

   ¼ teaspoon crushed, dried red peppers

Select the vegetables desired from the list, using at least five for variety. Place in a glass or ceramic bowl.

Combine the oil, lemon juice, vinegar, sugar, salt, oregano, and peppers in a 2-cup glass jar with a lid. Shake vigorously to blend. Pour over the vegetables. Let marinate at room temperature at least 1 hour; stir occasionally. Drain before serving.

Makes 8 or more servings.

Fresh Vegetables:

    Cauliflower florets
    Broccoli florets
    Cherry tomatoes
    Thinly sliced carrot rounds
    Thinly sliced cucumber rounds
    Thinly sliced zucchini rounds
    Small whole mushrooms
    Thinly sliced red onions, separated into rings

SANGRITA ASPIC

A surprising combination of well-spiced tomato juice and orange juice.

3 envelopes unflavored gelatin

3 cups tomato juice

4 teaspoons Worcestershire sauce

2 teaspoons salt

½ teaspoon onion salt

⅛ teaspoon Tabasco sauce

4 tablespoons lemon juice

1½ cups orange juice

Combine the gelatin and 1 cup of the tomato juice in a saucepan. Heat and stir until the gelatin is dissolved.

Remove from the heat and stir in the remaining 2 cups tomato juice, Worcestershire sauce, salt, onion salt, and Tabasco sauce. Then stir in the lemon juice and orange juice.

Pour into a 5-cup lightly oiled mold. Chill until firm. Unmold and serve with mayonnaise.

Makes 12 or more servings.

SHERRIED BING CHERRY SALAD

A perfect solution when a sweet molded salad is in order. Sherry gives it a delicious flavor.

1   can (17 ounces) dark sweet cherries (pitted)

¼   cup broken pecan halves

1   package (3 ounces) black-cherry-flavored gelatin

¼   cup dry sherry

    Watercress sprigs, for garnish

½   cup heavy cream, whipped

Drain the cherries, reserving the syrup. Insert a piece of pecan in the cavity of each cherry.

If necessary, add enough water to the cherry syrup to make 1 cup of liquid; then bring to a boil. Remove from the heat and add the gelatin; stir until dissolved.

Pour ¼ cup sherry into a 1-cup measure; add any remaining cherry syrup and enough water to make 1 cup total liquid. Stir into the gelatin mixture. Chill until thickened. Fold in the cherries.

Pour into a lightly oiled 3- to 4-cup ring mold. Chill until firm.

Unmold onto a serving plate. Garnish the outer edge with watercress sprigs. Place a small bowl of whipped cream in the center (lightly sweetened and flavored with vanilla, if desired).

Makes 6 servings.

SEAFOAM SALAD

A perfect blend of pears, lime gelatin, and whipped cream—a salad sweet enough to substitute as a dessert.

1 can (20 ounces) pears in syrup

1 package (3 ounces) lime-flavored gelatin

2 tablespoons mayonnaise

2 packages (3 ounces each) cream cheese, softened

1 cup heavy cream, whipped

Drain the pears, reserving 1 cup of the syrup. Heat the syrup to boiling; add the gelatin and stir until dissolved. Chill until syrupy.

Blend the mayonnaise into the softened cream cheese. Gradually stir in the gelatin mixture; stir until smooth.

Mash the pears to a pulp with a fork, or use a food processor. Add to the cream cheese mixture; blend. Fold in the whipped cream. Spoon into a lightly oiled 6-cup mold; chill until firm. Unmold onto a serving plate.

Makes 8 or more servings.

Note: This recipe may be doubled easily. For a special presentation, surround the mold with additional canned pear halves. Fill the cavities with puffs of whipped cream and green, candied cherry halves. Place sprigs of watercress between the pears.

PINEAPPLE SALAD MOLD

Similar to the previous salad, but pineapple, rather than pears, provides the flavor.

2 envelopes unflavored gelatin

1 cup cold water

1 cup sugar

1 can (20 ounces) crushed pineapple

2 packages (3 ounces each) cream cheese, at room temperature

2 cups light cream

Sprinkle the gelatin over the cold water in a saucepan. Add the sugar; cook and continue stirring until the gelatin and sugar are dissolved. Remove from the heat and stir in the pineapple (with the juices). Let stand until cool.

Beat the cream cheese until smooth; then gradually stir in the cream. Gradually stir into the gelatin mixture.

Pour into a lightly oiled 6-cup mold; chill until firm. Unmold onto a serving plate.

Makes 8 or more servings.

Note: For an attractive garnish, surround the mold with half slices of canned pineapple (edges rolled in finely chopped parsley), with a candied or maraschino cherry in the center of each.

MARINATED MANDARIN ORANGES

Made colorful with ruby-red pomegranate seeds. Especially appropriate when roast turkey is the star of the cold buffet.

2 cans (16 ounces each) mandarin oranges

¼ cup curaçao or other orange-flavored liqueur

1 fresh pomegranate

Drain the mandarin oranges. Place in a bowl and add the curaçao. Chill several hours or overnight.

Cut the pomegranate in half. Carefully dislodge the seeds with a small cocktail fork or nut pick. Chill.

When ready to serve, sprinkle the pomegranate seeds over the oranges; mix in carefully.

Make 4 cups.

ROASTED PEPPERS

An especially attractive dish if both red and green peppers are used.

4 large green peppers (or 2 red and 2 green)

1 clove garlic, finely chopped

Salt

Pepper

4½ tablespoons olive oil

1½ tablespoons wine vinegar

2 tablespoons parsley, finely chopped

Lemon wedges, for garnish

Place the peppers under a hot broiler. When the skin is partially charred on one side, turn another side toward the flame. Repeat until all the skin is well blistered and charred. Remove the peppers and place in a brown paper bag for about 10 minutes. (The collected moisture will soften the skins and make them easier to peel.) Using your fingers, peel away the skins.

Cut the peppers into lengthwise strips, about ¾- to 1-inch wide, removing the seeded core and trimming away the thick membrane.

Arrange the strips of pepper in spoke fashion on a serving plate. Sprinkle with the garlic, salt and pepper (lightly), olive oil, and vinegar.

Refrigerate for 4 hours or longer, then bring to room temperature before serving. Sprinkle the parsley over the top, then garnish the plate with lemon wedges.

Makes 8 or more servings.

FROSTED BEETS

Tiny beets with a horseradish cream topping; an attractive garnish for a cold meat platter, or a dish that can stand alone.

1 can (16 ounces) small whole beets

¼ cup sour cream

1 tablespoon prepared horseradish, well drained

Parsley, finely chopped, for garnish

Drain the beets, then dry well on paper toweling. Cut the larger beets in half (there is a mix of sizes in the can), but leave the small ones whole. Trim a slice off the top of each to hold the filling, and another from the bottom (large beets too) so that they have a base for standing upright when served.

Combine the sour cream and horseradish. Spread the flat tops of the beets with the mixture, making rounded mounds. Sprinkle with a few parsley flakes for color. Chill.

Makes about 2 dozen.

Note: The beets should not be frosted more than an hour or so in advance, as the juice from the beets will bleed into the edges of the frosting, turning them pink.

ARTICHOKE HEARTS VINAIGRETTE

These artichokes may be prepared and served in an hour or so, or kept for days.

2 **cans (14 ounces each) artichoke hearts in brine**

1 **teaspoon salt**

1 **teaspoon dry mustard**

1 **teaspoon dried tarragon, crumbled**

1 **tablespoon fresh parsley, finely chopped**

1 **clove garlic, peeled and split**

2 **tablespoons white wine vinegar**

6 **tablespoons olive oil**

Drain the artichokes; rinse with cold water, then drain again. Cut into bite-size pieces—fourths or sixths, depending on size. Place in a nonmetal mixing bowl.

In a separate small bowl, combine the salt, dry mustard, tarragon, parsley, and garlic. Gradually add the vinegar, then the olive oil; beat well with a fork. Pour over the artichokes. Let marinate at room temperature at least an hour, or several hours if desired. Remove the garlic before serving in the marinade.

Makes about 2 cups.

Note: These marinated artichokes keep well, refrigerated. (The garlic should be removed as directed.) Bring to room temperature before serving.

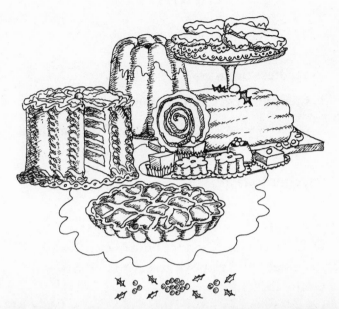

ḦOLIDAY SWEETS

Among the sweets included here are the traditional favorites such as Bûche de Noël, a chocolate cake roll decorated to represent the Yule log of Christmas past; Pound Cake made with sour cream; Nesselrode Pie with candied fruits and nuts dotted through the airy filling; unbaked Stained-Glass Window Fruitcake; and Ambrosia, the Southern must, made with fresh pineapple, coconut, and oranges. Other special desserts are a six-layer Hazelnut Torte filled with whipped cream; fresh Strawberry Meringue Torte; and Baba au Rhum, the famous yeast-raised rum cake from France. Among the finger foods are Petits Fours with Port Wine Glaze; Lemon Squares, a pastry with a creamy tart topping; and easily made Lady Finger Eclairs, with a crème de menthe filling and chocolate glaze.

149

AMBROSIA

A Southern favorite for the Christmas holidays.

> 8 seedless oranges
> 1 medium-size fresh pineapple
> 4 cups freshly grated or canned coconut, loosely
>   packed (see note)
>   Sugar to taste

Peel the oranges, removing all the spongy white part. Cut in half from the blossom end; cut into ¼-inch slices.

Peel the pineapple; remove the core and discard. Cut the flesh into bite-size chunks.

Arrange a layer of the orange slices in a large glass or crystal serving bowl. Sprinkle with a little sugar. Add a layer of grated coconut, then a layer of pineapple, sprinkling each with sugar (the amount will depend on the natural sweetness of the fruits). Continue the layers, ending with the coconut.

Cover and chill thoroughly, overnight if desired.

Makes 12 or more servings.

Note: To prepare a fresh coconut, puncture two of the eyes (soft spots) with a screwdriver. Drain and discard the liquid. Bake the coconut in a preheated 400° oven until it splits open, about 15 minutes. Cool, then break the coconut into several sections with a mallet. Pry the meat loose from the shell, if necessary. Trim off the brown skin using a vegetable peeler. Grate the coconut meat by hand, or use a food processor.

HOSPITALITY PLATTER

A whole pineapple, cut in quarters through the fronds, is arranged on a platter with fresh strawberries and with a bowl of powdered sugar for dipping. Simple, but spectacular.

1 **large fresh pineapple, with attractive fronds**

2 **pints fresh strawberries**

3 **tablespoons curaçao or other orange-flavored liqueur**

Confectioners' sugar

Trim the base end from the pineapple, then cut through lengthwise in half through the fronds. Cut each half in the same manner to make 4 sections.

Working with one section, slide a sharp knife close to the shell and remove the flesh in one piece. Place on a cutting board. Trim off the core, then split lengthwise; return to the shell, then score across into bite-size pieces. Cut the other sections in the same way. Chill if holding more than an hour or so, and score when ready to serve.

Rinse the strawberries in cold water briefly; dry on paper toweling. Do not remove the hulls. Place in a bowl and sprinkle the curaçao over them; turn to coat. Let stand 1 hour; drain. (This will sweeten the berries slightly and give them a dewy look.)

To serve, arrange the pineapple sections in a cross on a large, round platter with fronds extending over the edge. Place a small bowl of confectioners' sugar in the center, and group the strawberries between the pineapple quarters.
Makes 10 or more servings.

STRAWBERRIES ROMANOFF

Although this dessert requires some last minute preparation, it is easily put together, and always appreciated.

4 pints fresh strawberries

6 tablespoons sugar (or to taste)

1 pint French vanilla ice cream

1 cup heavy cream

¼ cup Cointreau

2 tablespoons cognac

2 tablespoons lemon juice

Several hours before serving, rinse the berries; drain well and remove the caps. Place in a nonmetallic bowl; add the sugar, turning the berries to coat, then refrigerate.

When ready to serve, turn the ice cream into a bowl. Beat until smooth. (If frozen solid, it may be necessary to soften in the refrigerator 10 to 20 minutes.)

Whip the cream until stiff, but not buttery; then fold into the ice cream until blended, along with the Cointreau, cognac, and lemon juice. Fold in the strawberries (with their juices). Turn into a serving bowl, preferably glass or crystal. Serve immediately.

Makes 12 to 16 servings.

VIENNESE STRAWBERRY TORTE

A magnificent dessert, easy to make. Layers of golden cake with chewy meringue joined by and topped with fresh strawberries. Whipped vanilla ice cream serves as a sauce.

½ cup (1 stick) butter

1½ cups sugar

4 eggs, separated

1⅓ cups sifted cake flour

1½ teaspoons baking powder

¼ teaspoon salt

5 tablespoons milk

½ teaspoon almond extract

⅛ teaspoon cream of tartar

3 pints small, fresh strawberries

½ cup sugar, to sweeten strawberries

1 pint vanilla ice cream

Cream the butter until soft. Gradually add ½ cup of the sugar and beat until light and fluffy. Add the egg yolks one at a time, beating well after each addition.

Sift the flour with the baking powder and salt three times. Add to the butter mixture alternately with the milk combined with the almond extract. (The batter will be stiff.) Spread in the bottoms of two greased and floured 8-inch round layer cake pans, having the mixture slightly higher on the sides than in the middle.

Beat the egg whites with the cream of tartar until soft

peaks form; then gradually beat in the remaining 1 cup sugar; beat until stiff and glossy. Spread and smooth evenly over the cake batter.

Bake in a preheated 350° oven for 30 to 35 minutes, or until the cake tests done and the meringue is set. Cool on racks before removing from the pans.

Rinse the strawberries and remove the hulls. Add the ½ cup sugar to 1 pint of the strawberries only and mix gently. Let stand, stirring occasionally, until a juice forms and the sugar is dissolved (20 to 30 minutes).

To serve, place one torte layer, meringue side up, on a serving plate. Cover with the sweetened strawberries. Add the second layer, also meringue side up. Cover the top with the whole strawberries.

Whip the ice cream until smooth, using an electric mixer set at high speed. Spoon a little over the strawberries, serving the remainder in a separate bowl as a sauce for individual servings.

Makes 8 to 10 servings.

Note: The torte layers may be made a day in advance; leave in the pans and cover tightly.

HAZELNUT TORTE

Six layers with lots of whipped cream. Rich but not overly sweet.

9 eggs, separated

1 teaspoon cream of tartar

1 cup sugar

1 tablespoon kirsch or light rum

Grated rind of 1 lemon

½ pound hazelnuts, ground

4 tablespoons fine, dry bread crumbs

½ teaspoon baking powder

Whipped Cream Topping (recipe follows)

Beat the egg whites with the cream of tartar until soft peaks form; gradually beat in ¼ cup of the sugar, a tablespoon at a time, until stiff peaks form.

Beat the egg yolks with the remaining ¾ cup of sugar until very thick and fluffy. Beat in the kirsch and lemon rind. Fold in the egg whites.

Combine the hazelnuts, bread crumbs, and baking powder. Fold in gently, but thoroughly.

Bake in three 9-inch greased and floured layer cake pans in a preheated 350° oven for 25 minutes, or until the layers begin to pull away from the sides of the pans. Cool before removing from pans.

Slit the layers horizontally to make 6 layers.

Fill and frost the top and sides with the Whipped Cream Topping. Refrigerate until ready to serve. May be made a

155

day in advance if desired. The torte layers may be made several days in advance and stored in covered tins.
Makes 10 to 12 servings.

WHIPPED CREAM TOPPING

    3 **cups heavy cream**

    ¾ **cup confectioners' sugar**

    2½ **teaspoons vanilla extract**

Whip the cream with the sugar and vanilla extract until stiff.

VENETIAN TORTE

*A beautiful dessert. Split layers of cake are filled and frosted alter-
nately with creamy chocolate and custard. The custard filling is spread
on the sides of the cake and garnished with sliced almonds; the top is
spread with the dark filling, then sprinkled with grated chocolate.
Hard work but worth it.*

    5 **eggs (1 cup)**

    1 **cup sugar**

  1/2 **teaspoon salt**

    1 **teaspoon vanilla extract**

1 1/4 **cups sifted all-purpose flour**

      Custard Cream (recipe follows)

      Chocolate Cream (recipe follows)

  1/2 **cup toasted, sliced unblanched almonds**

      Grated Chocolate Garnish (method follows)

Beat the eggs until light and fluffy. Use an electric mixer.
Gradually beat in the sugar, salt, and vanilla. Continue beating until thick and ivory colored, about 8 to 10 minutes.

Sift the flour, 2 tablespoons at a time, over the batter, fold-
ing in gently with a rubber spatula after each addition, then
gently but thoroughly with the last amount of flour.

Pour the batter into two greased 8 × 1 1/2-inch round cake
pans that have been lined on the bottoms with waxed paper.

Bake in a preheated 350° oven for 25 to 30 minutes. Cool
in the pans on racks. Ease gently out of the pans and peel off
the waxed paper. Using a long serrated knife, split each
layer in half to form two layers.

Place one layer, crust side down, on a serving plate.
Spread with the Custard Cream, using about one-fourth of

157

the total amount. Place a second layer on top, crust side up. Spread it with half the Chocolate Cream. Add the next layer, and as before, add one-fourth of the Custard Cream, the last layer (crust on top), and the remainder of the Chocolate Cream. Spread the remaining Custard Cream on the sides and press the sliced almonds into it for garnish. Top with the Chocolate Garnish. Chill.

Makes 10 to 12 servings.

Note: This torte may be made the day before serving.

CUSTARD CREAM

> ¾ **cup sugar**
>
> 2 **tablespoons cornstarch**
>
> 3 **eggs**
>
> 1½ **cups milk**
>
> ½ **cup (1 stick) butter, softened**
>
> 1 **teaspoon vanilla extract**

Combine the sugar and cornstarch in a saucepan. Add the eggs and beat until fluffy. Stir in the milk.

Cook, stirring constantly, over medium heat until thickened and smooth. Cool.

Beat the softened butter and vanilla into the cooled custard until smooth. Chill before using.

CHOCOLATE CREAM

> 1½ **cups sifted confectioners' sugar**
>
> ¼ **teaspoon salt**
>
> 1 **egg**
>
> 4 **tablespoons soft butter**
>
> 1½ **squares (1½ ounces) unsweetened chocolate, melted**

Combine the sugar, salt, egg, butter, and melted chocolate in a mixing bowl; beat until light and fluffy.

GRATED CHOCOLATE GARNISH

Using a vegetable peeler, scrape along the narrow side of a square of unsweetened chocolate, to form thin slivers. (Do this directly over the frosting, using enough to cover lightly.)

BÛCHE DE NOËL

*The Yule log of Christmas past is recreated with a chocolate cake roll,
which is filled, coated with a frosting that is striated to resemble the
bark, then garnished with chopped pistachios to suggest green moss.*

3 eggs

1 cup sugar

⅓ cup cold water

1 teaspoon vanilla extract

1 cup sifted cake flour

¼ cup unsweetened dry cocoa

1 teaspoon baking powder

¼ teaspoon salt

Confectioners' sugar

Mocha Butter Cream (recipe follows)

Whipped Cream Topping (recipe follows)

Pistachios, finely chopped, for garnish

Beat the eggs in a large bowl with an electric mixer at high
speed until light and fluffy. Gradually beat in the sugar and
continue to beat until thick and pale, about 8 to 10 minutes.
Stir in the water and vanilla.

Sift the flour with the cocoa, baking powder, and salt.
Fold into the egg mixture.

Grease a 15 × 10 × 1-inch jelly roll pan; line the bottom
with waxed paper and grease the paper. Pour in the batter
and spread evenly.

Bake in a preheated 375° oven for 12 to 15 minutes, or
until the center springs back when lightly pressed.

Loosen the cake around the edges with a knife, then invert the pan onto a towel dusted with confectioners' sugar. Peel off the waxed paper. Trim the edges of the cake for easier rolling. Roll up from the long side with the towel, jelly roll fashion. Cool.

When the cake is completely cool, carefully unroll and spread evenly with the Mocha Butter Cream. Reroll and place in refrigerator; chill at least 24 hours.

An hour or more before serving, spread the log with the Whipped Cream Topping. Use the tines of a fork to create a bark-like appearance. Sprinkle the top (at the ends only) with the chopped pistachios, to resemble moss. Chill until ready to serve.

Makes 8 to 10 servings.

MOCHA BUTTER CREAM

    1 **cup (2 sticks) sweet butter, softened**

    ¼ **cup sifted confectioners' sugar**

    1 **tablespoon instant coffee dissolved in 1½ teaspoons hot water**

    2 **egg whites**

Beat the butter with the sugar until light and fluffy. Blend in the dissolved coffee; then beat in the egg whites until the mixture is smooth.

WHIPPED CREAM TOPPING

    1 **cup heavy cream**

    ¼ **cup sifted confectioners' sugar**

    ¼ **cup unsweetened dry cocoa**

    4 **tablespoons crème de cacao (light or dark)**

Whip the cream until it begins to thicken. Gradually beat in the sugar, cocoa, and crème de cacao, beating until the cream stands in firm peaks.

PAVÉ AU CHOCOLAT

A fancy loaf cake quickly put together with lady fingers and rich chocolate frosting.

¾ cup (1½ sticks) butter, at room temperature

1 cup sifted confectioners' sugar

4 egg yolks

4 squares (1 ounce each) unsweetened chocolate, melted and cooled

3 tablespoons kirsch or rum

½ cup cold water

24 double lady fingers

Slivered toasted almonds, for garnish (optional)

Cream the butter with the confectioners' sugar. Stir in the egg yolks, one at a time; then blend in the melted chocolate. Set aside.

Combine the kirsch with the water in a deep bowl. One at a time, quickly dip 8 of the lady fingers (do not split) in and out of the liquid. Arrange them in a row, with sides touching, on an oblong serving platter.

Spread a layer of the chocolate mixture on top. Repeat the procedure with the remaining lady fingers to make a three-tiered loaf. Frost the sides and top with the remaining chocolate. Garnish the top with the almonds. Refrigerate at least 3 hours, but bring to room temperature before serving.
Makes 8 servings.

POUND CAKE

It wouldn't be Christmas without pound cake to serve along with traditional eggnog. This is an unusual version made with sour cream.

1 cup (2 sticks) butter

1 teaspoon vanilla extract

3 cups sugar

6 eggs

3 cups sifted all-purpose flour

¼ teaspoon baking soda

½ teaspoon salt

1 cup sour cream

In a large bowl of an electric mixer, cream the butter. Add the vanilla and gradually add the sugar. Beat until light.

Add the eggs, one at a time, beating well after each addition.

Sift the flour with the soda and salt. Add half to the egg mixture, then add the sour cream, and the remaining dry ingredients. Beat only until smooth after each addition.

Turn the batter into a greased and floured 9- to 10-inch tube pan. Bake in a preheated 350° oven for about 1½ hours, or until a cake tester comes out dry.

Turn out immediately and cool right side up on a rack.

Makes at least 16 servings.

Note: For best flavor wrap and store a day before serving. This cake keeps well.

GERMAN HOLIDAY CAKE

Brandy, lemon, and almonds blend to provide this cake with an un-forgettable flavor.

1 cup (2 sticks) unsalted butter

1½ cups sugar

4 eggs

3 tablespoons light cream

2¼ cups sifted cake flour

2 teaspoons baking powder

½ teaspoon salt

¼ cup brandy

2 tablespoons lemon juice

1 tablespoon lemon rind, grated

1 cup blanched almonds, finely chopped

Confectioners' sugar

Cream the butter, using an electric mixer. Add the sugar and beat until very light. Beat in the eggs one at a time, beating well after each addition. Beat in the cream.

Sift the flour, baking powder, and salt. Combine the brandy and lemon juice. Add the flour mixture alternately with the brandy mixture, beginning and ending with the dry ingredients. Blend only until smooth after each addition.

Remove from the mixer and fold in the lemon rind and almonds, using a rubber spatula.

Turn the batter into a greased and floured 9-inch tube pan. Level the top.

Bake in a preheated 350° oven for 55 to 60 minutes, or until the cake pulls away from the sides and a pick comes out clean.

Cool 20 minutes on a rack, then turn out and cool completely, right side up. Wrap and store overnight before serving.

Dust with sifted confectioners' sugar when ready to serve. *Makes 12 or more servings.*

Note: If an angel food cake pan is used (with high center tube), remove the cake from the outside part of the pan; loosen the bottom and around the tube; let stand until cool before removing.

BABA AU RHUM

Featured in both French and Italian cuisines, this yeast cake is complete only when saturated with a rum syrup. Some like it with unsweetened whipped cream.

    1 **cup milk**

    3 **cakes compressed yeast (see note)**

3¾ **cups sifted all-purpose flour**

    1 **cup (2 sticks) butter**

  ¾ **cup superfine sugar**

    5 **eggs, at room temperature**

  ¼ **teaspoon salt**

    1 **cup currants**

        Grated rind of ½ lemon

        Rum Syrup (recipe follows)

        Unsweetened whipped cream (optional)

Heat the milk until lukewarm (90°). Crumble in the yeast; stir to dissolve. Sift in 1 cup of the flour; stir to incorporate. Cover and let stand in a warm place until doubled, about 1½ hours.

Cream the butter with the sugar until very light. Add the eggs, one at a time, beating in each one thoroughly; add the salt. Combine with the raised mixture.

Toss the currants in 1 tablespoon flour; add along with the lemon rind to the batter. Sift in the remaining 2¾ cups flour. Beat until the batter is elastic and smooth. Place in a

Note: *You may substitute 3 packages of dry yeast. Dissolve in warm milk (110°).*

well-buttered 9-inch tube pan. Cover and let rise to top of the pan, about 1¼ to 1½ hours.

Bake in a preheated 350° oven for 40 to 50 minutes. Test with a wooden pick. Remove to a serving platter and gradually drip the rum syrup onto the warm cake so that the syrup soaks in. Cool before serving. Cut into wedges and serve with unsweetened cream if desired.

Makes 1 large baba to serve 8 to 12.

Note: The baba keeps a week beautifully.

RUM SYRUP

> 1 **cup sugar**
>
> ½ **cup water**
>
> 1 **lemon, thinly sliced**
>
> **Pinch of salt**
>
> ½ **cup light rum**

Combine the sugar, water, lemon slices, and salt in a saucepan. Cook over low heat, stirring until the sugar dissolves. Then boil gently for 10 to 15 minutes, or until of light syrupy consistency (220°). Cool slightly; remove the lemon slices and add the rum. Cool.

STAINED-GLASS WINDOW
FRUITCAKE

A fruitcake—actually a confection—that requires no baking.

1 **package (7 ounces) pitted dates**

½ **package (15 ounces) raisins**

3 **tablespoons orange juice**

2 **tablespoons lemon juice**

6 **candied pineapple rings (2 red, 2 green, 2 yellow)**

3 **ounces candied citron, coarsely chopped**

9 **ounces mixed candied fruit**

8 **ounces pecan halves**

Put the dates and raisins through a food chopper, or use a food processor, to cut fine. Add the orange juice and lemon juice; mix lightly with a fork.

Thinly slice the candied pineapple rings. Add to the date-raisin mixture, along with the citron, candied fruit, and pecans. With buttered hands, knead until the ingredients are well distributed.

Pack tightly into a 5-cup ring mold which has been lined with aluminum foil. Pat down until smooth. Cover and refrigerate at least 3 days before serving. (It will keep for several weeks.)

To serve, turn out of the mold. Decorate in any manner that seems appropriate. Serve cold, thinly sliced.
Makes 1 large ring.

Note: For a special presentation, set the ring of fruitcake on a platter with a lighted candle in the center. A thinly cut slice when held close to the flame will give the effect of a light shining through a colorful stained-glass window.

MERINGUES WITH GLAZED WALNUTS

Individual foam cakes, as they are known in Germany, are filled with orange-flavored whipped cream, then garnished with scrapings of orange rind and sweet, toasted walnut halves.

> 6 egg whites (¾ cup)
>
> 2 cups superfine sugar
>
> 1½ teaspoons white vinegar
>
> 1 cup heavy cream
>
> 2 tablespoons curaçao or other orange-flavored liqueur
>
> Grated orange rind
>
> Glazed Walnuts (recipe follows)

Beat the egg whites until soft peaks form. Gradually beat in 1 cup of the sugar (add slowly or the meringues will be granular). Gradually add the remaining 1 cup of sugar alternately with the vinegar, beating until the sugar is completely dissolved.

Cut 2 pieces of heavy brown paper to fit 2 large baking sheets. Mark eight 3-inch circles (1½ inches apart) on each paper. Drop a generous spoonful of meringue into the center of each. With the bowl of a teaspoon, spread to the edges of the circles, hollowing out the center of each to form a cavity.

Bake in a preheated 225° oven for 1 to 1¼ hours, or until dried and crisp. Cool on the paper, then remove with a spatula. (These may be made weeks in advance and stored in a loosely covered container.)

When ready to serve (or up to 2 hours in advance), whip the cream with the curaçao until stiff. Fill the meringue shells. Grate a few slivers of orange rind over the top of each and garnish with 3 or 4 glazed walnuts.
Makes 16 servings.

GLAZED WALNUTS

- 2 **cups walnut halves**
- 4 **cups boiling water**
- 3 **tablespoons sugar**
- **Oil, for deep frying**

Place the walnuts in a bowl; pour the boiling water over them and let stand 3 minutes; drain. Immediately add the sugar, stirring well to coat. Spread out on waxed paper and let stand overnight to dry.

Put half the walnuts in a large wire strainer. Dip in and out of oil, heated to 325°, until brown and crisp. Drain on paper toweling briefly, then loosen with your hands to prevent sticking as they cool. Repeat with the remainder. Store in a tightly covered container.

Note: More walnuts than are required in the recipe are called for. Serve the remainder as a cocktail tidbit.

HOLIDAY SOUFFLÉ

This cold mousse is molded in a soufflé dish and ends up looking like a well-risen, baked soufflé. The ingredients—cherries, currants, and pecans—are typical of the Christmas season.

1 envelope unflavored gelatin

¼ cup milk

¾ cup sugar

4 egg whites

Pinch of salt

1 cup heavy cream

1½ teaspoons vanilla extract

¼ cup maraschino cherries, chopped and well drained

¼ cup currants

¼ cup pecans, chopped

Prepare a 3-cup soufflé dish by pinning or tying a folded piece of aluminum foil around the dish so that it extends 1½ inches above the rim. The foil and dish should be lightly oiled.

In a small saucepan, combine the gelatin, milk, and ½ cup of the sugar. Stir over very low heat until the gelatin and sugar are dissolved. Remove and set aside to cool.

Beat the egg whites with the salt until soft peaks form. Beat in the remaining ¼ cup sugar, a tablespoon at a time; beat just until glossy.

Whip the cream with the vanilla just until it mounds gently.

Gradually fold the cooled gelatin mixture into the egg

whites, and then gradually fold that into the whipped cream. Sprinkle the cherries, currants, and pecans over the top; fold in. Spoon the mousse into the soufflé dish and chill until firm, at least 4 hours.

Before serving the mousse, unfasten the collar and peel it away carefully.

Makes 6 to 8 servings.

Note: For a special presentation, decorate the sides of the soufflé (which extend above the dish) with finely chopped pecans. Hold the dish in one hand over a bowl containing the nuts; scoop up the nuts with the other hand and press against the sides. Pipe small rosettes of whipped cream around the top and place half a cherry on each. (Reserve a little of the cream from the basic recipe; it should be whipped stiff.)

NESSELRODE PIE

A perfect pie for the holidays: rum-flavored chiffon filling with al-monds, raisins, and candied fruits.

1 envelope plus 1 teaspoon unflavored gelatin

½ cup sugar

½ teaspoon salt

1¼ cups milk

3 eggs, separated

¼ cup light rum

1 cup heavy cream

⅓ cup diced, mixed candied fruit

2 tablespoons blanched almonds, chopped

1 tablespoon raisins, chopped

A 9-inch baked pastry shell (see note)

Combine the gelatin with ¼ cup of the sugar and the salt in the top of a double boiler. Gradually stir in the milk. Cook over simmering water until the gelatin has dissolved.

Beat the egg yolks slightly, then gradually stir in the gelatin mixture; return to the double boiler. Cook, stirring constantly, until the mixture coats a spoon and is slightly thickened. Remove from the heat, pour into a bowl and chill. Stir occasionally until the mixture mounds slightly when dropped from a spoon. Beat in the rum, just until smooth.

Beat the egg whites until soft peaks form; then gradually beat in the remaining ¼ cup sugar. Continue beating until stiff and glossy. Fold into the gelatin mixture.

Whip the cream until it mounds softly. Fold into the gelatin mixture; then fold in the mixed candied fruit, almonds, and raisins.

Turn into the cooled pastry shell and chill until set. Remove from the refrigerator 20 minutes before serving.

Makes 8 servings.

Note: Prepare pastry (see page 95) for a 9-inch shell. Flute the edges with your fingers. Prick the pastry thoroughly with a fork to prevent puffing during baking. Bake in a preheated 400° oven for 10 to 12 minutes, or until golden brown. Check after 5 minutes. If the pastry puffs up, prick again 2 or 3 times to release the air. Cool on a rack. Brush with melted butter and refrigerate to set before filling. This will help prevent a soggy crust.

GRASSHOPPER PIE

Delicious—just like the drink.

1½ teaspoons unflavored gelatin

⅓ cup milk

¼ cup sugar

4 egg yolks

¼ cup green crème de menthe

¼ cup white crème de cacao

1 cup heavy cream, whipped

Chocolate Cookie Crust (recipe follows)

Chocolate Scrolls, for garnish (method follows)

Sprinkle the gelatin over the milk in a heavy saucepan. When softened, add the sugar and egg yolks; stir to blend. Place over low heat and stir until the gelatin and sugar dissolve and the mixture thickens. (Do not boil.) Remove from the heat.

Stir in the crème de menthe and crème de cacao. Strain through a wire sieve into a large bowl and chill until the mixture starts to thicken.

Stir in a little of the whipped cream to lighten the mixture, then fold in the remainder.

Turn the mixture into the cooled Chocolate Cookie Crust. Chill until firm, several hours or overnight.

Cut into wedges for serving, garnishing each with a Chocolate Scroll.

Makes 8 servings.

Note: The recipe may be doubled to serve 16. The doubled ingredients for the filling may be prepared together.

CHOCOLATE COOKIE CRUST

    1½ **cups fine, chocolate cookie crumbs (from**
          wafers)

    ¼ **cup sugar**

    ¼ **cup melted butter**

Combine the cookie crumbs, sugar, and melted butter. Press into the bottom and sides of a 9-inch buttered pie plate.

Bake in a preheated 350° oven for 10 minutes; cool.

CHOCOLATE SCROLLS

Let a square of semisweet chocolate stand in a warm place until warm. (An unlit oven is ideal.) Draw a vegetable peeler over the flat side to make a scroll; repeat to make 8 scrolls. Do this over a plate; let stand in a cool place until firm, then transfer to the pie with a spatula.

SWEDISH MAZARINS

Rich, fluted tart shells with almond macaroon centers, best served slightly warm.

> 4 ounces (about ½ cup) almond paste (see note)
>
> ⅓ cup butter, softened
>
> 2 eggs
>
> ¼ teaspoon almond extract
>
> Mazarin Pastry (recipe follows)
>
> ¼ cup sifted confectioners' sugar
>
> 2 teaspoons dry sherry

Crumble the almond paste into a mixing bowl. Add the butter and blend until smooth. Add the eggs and almond extract; beat until smooth and light.

Spoon the filling into the tart pans, lined with Mazarin Pastry. Place on a baking sheet; then bake in a preheated 350° oven for 20 to 25 minutes, or until the filling is firm and golden brown.

Cool until the tarts can be handled, then remove and cool on racks. Dribble with icing made by blending the confectioners' sugar with the sherry.

Makes 16 tarts.

Note: The tarts are best when freshly made and served while barely warm. They may be made several hours in advance and reheated slightly.

Almond paste may be purchased in the gourmet section in many supermarkets.

MAZARIN PASTRY

> ½ cup (1 stick) butter, softened
>
> ¼ cup sifted confectioners' sugar
>
> 1 egg yolk
>
> 1 cup sifted all-purpose flour

Cream the softened butter with the sugar. Stir in the egg yolk; then blend in the flour. Chill the dough about 20 minutes, or until it can be handled easily.

Divide into 16 equal balls. Press each into a 3- to 3½-inch tart pan (preferably fluted), covering the bottom and sides evenly.

ALMOND PASTRY

A two-layered crisp pastry glazed and sprinkled with toasted slivered almonds. Unusual and easily made.

BASIC PASTRY

    1 **cup unsifted all-purpose flour**

    ½ **cup shortening (part butter preferred)**

    2 **tablespoons cold water**

CREAM PUFF PASTRY

    ½ **cup (1 stick) butter**

    1 **cup water**

    1 **cup unsifted all-purpose flour**

    3 **eggs**

    ½ **teaspoon almond extract**

GLAZE

    1 **cup sifted confectioners' sugar**

    2 **tablespoons soft butter**

    1 **teaspoon vanilla extract**

    1 **tablespoon milk (about)**

    ½ **cup toasted slivered almonds**

To make the basic pastry, place the flour in a mixing bowl. Add the shortening; cut in with a pastry blender to form fine crumbs. Sprinkle the water over the mixture, mixing with a fork until it can be gathered into a ball. Divide in half.

Using an ungreased baking sheet, pat each half into a 12 × 3-inch strip, leaving 3 inches between the two.

To make the cream puff pastry, bring the butter and water to a rolling boil in a large saucepan, stirring until the butter is melted. Turn the heat to low; add the flour all at once and stir vigorously with a wooden spoon until the mixture leaves the sides of the pan. Remove from the heat. Add the eggs, one at a time, beating until smooth after each addition. Beat in the almond extract.

Spread this mixture over the pastry strips, dividing it evenly.

Bake in a preheated 350° oven for about 60 minutes, or until crisp and golden brown. Do not remove from the baking sheet.

To make the glaze, combine the confectioners' sugar butter, and vanilla. Add enough milk to make a smooth mixture. Spread over the tops of the warm pastries; then sprinkle with the almonds. Serve warm preferably, or cool completely.

Makes 10 to 12 servings.

Note: This pastry must be served the day it is baked. It may be frozen plain, then reheated slightly, adding the glaze and topping when warm.

SCOTCH SHORTBREAD

A traditional favorite to serve along with eggnog or other sweet punches. The dough, rich and buttery, is pressed into a round pan for baking, then cut into wedges for serving.

2 cups sifted all-purpose flour

½ cup sugar

1 cup (2 sticks) cold sweet butter

Sugar, for garnish

Combine the flour and sugar in a mixing bowl. Slice the cold butter into the flour mixture. Mix with your fingertips or a pastry blender to form coarse crumbs. Knead with your hands until the dough is smooth. Divide the dough into two equal portions.

Press each into an 8-inch round layer cake pan, smoothing the tops with a spatula. Prick the entire surface with a fork (as for pastry shells).

Bake in a preheated 300° oven for 45 minutes, or until faintly colored. Remove from the oven and sprinkle the tops lightly with sugar.

Cool on wire racks for 10 minutes; then cut each shortbread into 16 wedges. Let stand in the pans until completely cooled.

Makes 32 thin wedges.

LEMON SQUARES

Easily made shortbread pastries with a luscious lemon topping.

SHORTBREAD PASTRY

> 2 **cups sifted all-purpose flour**
>
> ½ **cup sugar**
>
> 1 **cup (2 sticks) butter, softened**

LEMON TOPPING

> 4 **eggs**
>
> 2 **cups sugar**
>
> ¼ **cup unsifted all-purpose flour**
>
> 1 **teaspoon baking powder**
>
> ½ **cup lemon juice**
>
> **Confectioners' sugar**

For the pastry, combine the flour and sugar. Work in the butter with a pastry blender or a fork until it forms a dough. Spread on the bottom of an ungreased 15 × 10 × 1-inch jelly roll pan. Pat the dough evenly with your hands, working it up about ½ inch at the edges.

Bake in a preheated 375° oven for 20 minutes. Remove from the oven.

For the topping, beat the eggs well. Add the sugar, flour, baking powder, and lemon juice; blend well.

Pour over the pastry (as soon as it is removed from the oven). Return to the 375° oven and bake 25 minutes longer. Remove and sprinkle the top lightly with confectioners' sugar. Cool in the pan, then cut into 1½-inch bite-size squares.

Makes 6 dozen pastry squares.

TOFFEE BARS

Thin crisp cookies with a coating of chocolate and finely chopped walnuts.

- 1 cup (2 sticks) butter or margarine
- 1 cup dark brown sugar (packed)
- 1 egg yolk
- 1 teaspoon vanilla extract
- 2 cups unsifted all-purpose flour
- 1 bar (8 ounces) milk chocolate, broken into quarters
- 1 cup walnuts, finely chopped

Cream the butter and brown sugar until light. Add the egg yolk and vanilla; blend. Gradually add the flour; mix well to form a dough.

Press the dough evenly over the bottom of an ungreased 15 × 10 × 1-inch jelly roll pan (use your fingers).

Bake in a preheated 375° oven for 20 minutes, or until firm and golden brown.

Remove the pan from the oven and immediately place the sections of the chocolate bar on top. As they begin to melt, spread evenly over the surface. Sprinkle with the chopped walnuts; press lightly so they adhere.

Cool slightly, but cut into bars while still warm (about 2 × 1-inch size). Then cool before removing from the pan.
Makes 6 dozen bars.

MOR MONSEN'S TEA CAKES

Norwegian tea cakes, traditionally cut into diamond shapes. The topping, a combination of currants, chopped almonds, and coarse sparkling sugar, is baked along with the batter.

¾ cup (1½ sticks) butter

¾ cup sugar

1 tablespoon lemon juice

2 teaspoons lemon rind, grated

4 eggs

1⅓ cups sifted all-purpose flour

½ teaspoon baking powder

¼ cup blanched almonds, chopped

¼ cup currants

¼ cup pearl sugar (see note)

Cream the butter. Gradually beat in the sugar; beat until light and fluffy. Blend in the lemon juice and rind.

Add the eggs, one at a time, beating well after each addition.

Sift the flour with the baking powder; blend into the batter.

Spread the mixture in a 13 × 9 × ¾-inch pan that has been greased and floured on the bottom. Combine the almonds and currants; sprinkle evenly over the dough.

Bake in a preheated 375° oven for 15 minutes; sprinkle the pearl sugar over the top. Continue baking about 10 minutes longer, or until golden brown. Cool in the pan.

For diamond shapes, cut diagonally across the pan at 2-inch intervals. Then repeat, cutting in the opposite direction. *Makes about 2 dozen small cakes.*

Note: Pearl sugar (or crystal sugar) crystals are coarse and irregular. The sugar may be purchased in German and Scandinavian specialty shops. Although not as attractive, crushed lump sugar may be substituted.

FRENCH CHOCOLATE CAKES

Miniature chocolate coated chocolate cakes—deliciously moist, incredibly rich.

6 tablespoons sweet butter, at room temperature

½ cup sugar

3 eggs, separated

2 tablespoons flour

4 squares (1 ounce each) unsweetened chocolate, melted

⅛ teaspoon salt

Chocolate Glaze (recipe follows)

Using a wire whisk, whip the butter, then gradually add the sugar. When blended, add the egg yolks, one at a time, whipping until well blended and slightly thickened. Fold in the flour; then stir in the melted chocolate.

Beat the egg whites with the salt until stiff, but still moist. Stir about one-third into the chocolate mixture until blended; fold in the remainder.

Spoon the batter into 24 well-buttered miniature muffin tins (measuring 1½-inches across the top). The batter is stiff and the pans will be heaping; it is not necessary to level the batter, as it will settle as it bakes.

Place one of the filled pans on a baking sheet. Bake in a preheated 325° oven for about 8 minutes. The outsides should feel slightly firm; the centers will feel dry, but soft. Do not overbake; the centers will firm as the cakes cool. Remove from the baking sheet, but cool in the pans. Repeat the process with the second pan.

When cool, remove and place inverted on a sheet of waxed paper.

While the cakes are cooling, prepare the Chocolate Glaze. When it has cooled to proper consistency for dipping (not quite spreadable), dip each cake into the glaze, turning to coat completely. Place inverted on the waxed paper and let stand until the glaze has hardened. (The bottoms will take longer than the top and sides; when hardened, the cakes will peel off the paper easily.)

Store at room temperature. Since they are completely sealed by the glaze, these cakes may be made several days in advance.

Makes 24 miniature cakes.

CHOCOLATE GLAZE

> 3 squares (1 ounce each) semisweet chocolate
>
> 1 teaspoon sweet butter
>
> 3 tablespoons Grand Marnier or other orange-
>   flavored liqueur

Melt the chocolate with the butter in a small saucepan set in a small skillet of simmering water. Remove from the heat and stir in the Grand Marnier. Let stand until a proper consistency for dipping. To hurry the process, set the pan in a bowl of ice water; stir constantly.

CHOCOLATE MINT STICKS

Mint-flavored brownies with a sugar glaze and a drizzle of melted chocolate on top.

>   2 eggs
>   1 cup sugar
>   ¼ teaspoon salt
>   ½ cup (1 stick) butter
>   1 square (1 ounce) unsweetened chocolate
>   6 tablespoons unsifted flour
>   ½ cup pecans, chopped
>   ¾ teaspoon peppermint extract
>   **Peppermint Glaze (recipe follows)**
>   **Melted Chocolate (method follows)**

Beat the eggs with the sugar and salt until fluffy.

Melt the butter and chocolate together in a small skillet over low heat; blend into the sugar mixture. Stir in the flour, pecans, and peppermint extract. Blend well, but do not beat.

Spread the batter in a greased 9 × 9 × 2-inch baking pan. Bake in a preheated 350° oven for 18 to 20 minutes. (Test in the center with a pick.) Cool in the pan on a wire rack.

Spread the Peppermint Glaze evenly over the top. When the glaze is set, drizzle the Melted Chocolate over the top in swirls to cover lightly. Refrigerate briefly to harden the toppings, then cut into bite-size strips.

Makes about 3 dozen strips.

PEPPERMINT GLAZE

    1½ tablespoons butter

    2 tablespoons light cream

    1½ cups confectioners' sugar

    ½ teaspoon peppermint extract

In a small skillet, melt the butter in the cream. Remove from heat and blend in the confectioners' sugar and peppermint extract.

MELTED CHOCOLATE

Melt 1 square (1 ounce) unsweetened chocolate with 1 teaspoon butter. Use while hot and thin.

PETITS FOURS WITH
PORT WINE GLAZE

Tiny rounds of chiffon cake are coated with a wine glaze, then deco-
rated with bits of candied cherries and citron.

2¼ cups sifted cake flour

1¼ cups sugar

   3 teaspoons baking powder

   1 teaspoon salt

  ⅓ cup vegetable oil

   1 cup milk

   2 eggs, separated

   1 teaspoon vanilla extract

     Port Wine Glaze (recipe follows)

     Red candied cherries and citron, for garnish

Sift the flour, 1 cup of the sugar, baking powder, and salt
into a large bowl of an electric mixer.

Blend in the vegetable oil and ½ cup of the milk; then
beat 2 minutes with mixer set at medium speed.

Blend in the egg yolks, the remaining ½ cup milk, and the
vanilla; beat 1 minute at medium speed.

In a separate bowl, beat the egg whites until soft peaks
form. Gradually add the remaining ¼ cup sugar, and continue beating until stiff. Fold meringue into the egg yolk
batter with a wire whisk until no streaks of white remain.

Pour the batter into a 15 × 10 × 1-inch jelly roll pan,
which has been lined on the bottom with greased waxed
paper.

Bake in a preheated 350° oven for 30 minutes, or until the top of the cake springs back when lightly pressed. Cool in the pan set on a wire rack.

Spread the top of the cooled cake with the Port Wine Glaze. When firm, cut the cake into rounds with a 1½-inch cutter. (To prevent drying, leave in place until ready to serve.)

Decorate the center of each cake with a tiny bit of candied cherry and place a sliver of citron on each side.

Makes 6 dozen petits fours.

Note: The cake may be wrapped securely and frozen; thaw wrapped. The glaze and decoration should be added the day of serving.

PORT WINE GLAZE

2⅔ **cups sifted confectioners' sugar**

4 **tablespoons port wine**

2 **tablespoons butter, melted**

Red food coloring

Combine the confectioners' sugar, port wine, and butter; blend well. Add a few drops of red food coloring to tint a light pink. Use immediately.

LADY FINGER ECLAIRS

Easily made replicas of the real thing. These eclairs are made with store-bought sponge cakes, filled with mint-flavored whipped cream, and then glazed with chocolate.

1/2 cup heavy cream

2 teaspoons confectioners' sugar

2 tablespoons green crème de menthe

18 double lady fingers

Chocolate Glaze (recipe follows)

Whip the cream with the confectioners' sugar until soft peaks form. Add the crème de menthe; whip until very stiff, but not buttery.

Cut the lady fingers apart with a sharp knife, then separate. Spread half generously with the whipped cream mixture, then cover with the remaining halves.

Using a table knife, spread the tops of each with a thick coating (not quite to the ends) of the Chocolate Glaze. (It should spread smoothly and look glossy; if not, add a few drops of hot water.)

Place the filled and glazed eclairs on a serving platter, then refrigerate until ready to serve—several hours in advance if desired. Remove long enough to allow the glaze to soften slightly before serving.

Makes 18 eclairs, or 9 servings.

CHOCOLATE GLAZE

1 square (1 ounce) unsweetened chocolate

1 tablespoon vegetable shortening

1/2 cup sifted confectioners' sugar

1 tablespoon hot water

1/4 teaspoon vanilla extract

Melt the chocolate with the shortening in a small saucepan over very low heat. Remove from the heat and blend in the sugar, hot water, and vanilla. Stir until smooth. (You should be able to use this glaze immediately.)

Almond
  and Cheese Spread, Toasted, 70
  Pastry, 180–81
Ambrosia, 150
Anchovy and Egg Turnovers, 98–99
Appetizers. *See* COLD CANAPES, DIPS
        AND SPREADS; HOT HORS
        D'OEUVRES
Artichoke Hearts
  with Avgolémono Sauce, 85–86
  Vinaigrette, 147
Aspic(s)
  Cold Chicken in, 110–11
  Sangrita, 140
  see also Daube Glacé, Glazed Cold
        Ham with Mustard Sauce,
        Jambon Persillé
Avgolémono Sauce, 86

Baba au Rhum, 167–68
Baked Crabmeat Spread, 94
Beans. *See* Black Beans, Green Beans
Beef
  Cold Roast Fillet of, 123–24
  see also Daube Glacé
Beets, Frosted, 146
Benedictine Canapés, 59–60
Beverages. *See* HOLIDAY PUNCHES AND
        DRINKS
Bing Cherry Salad, Sherried, 141
Biscuits, Cheese, 106
Bishop's Bread, 51
Bloody Marys, Perfect, 29
Blue Cheese Dip, Tangy, 66
Bohemian Hoska, 39
Bombay Punch, 24
Bread Slices, Toasted French, 80
Breads. *See* CHRISTMAS BREADS
Brown Bread, 55
Bûche de Noël, 160–62

Cake(s)
  French Chocolate, 187–88
  German Holiday, 165–66
  Pound, 164
  Tea, Mor Monson's, 185–86
  see also HOLIDAY SWEETS
Camembert Dip, Hot, 93
Canapés
  Benedictine, 59–60
  Hot
    Curried Cheese, 101
    Shrimp, 100
    see also COLD CANAPES, DIPS AND
        SPREADS; HOT HORS D'OEUVRES
Cardamom Braid, 36–37
Caviar, Red with Sour Cream, 72
Cheese
  and Toasted Almond Spread, 70
  Biscuits, 106
  Canapés, Hot Curried, 101
  Dip, Tangy Blue Cheese, 66
  Holiday, 131–32
  Jackets, Olives in, 103
  and Mushroom Salad, 133
  Potted Jack, 71
  on Rye, Toasted, 102
  see also Camembert Dip, Gateau
        Fromage, Quiche Lorraine
Cherries. *See* Bing Cherries
Chicken
  in Aspic, Cold, 110–11
  Tropicale, 112–13
Chicken Livers. *See* Country Pâté,
        Pâté d'Ascot, Rumaki
Chocolate, Pavé au, 163
Chocolate
  Cake Roll (Bûche De Noël), 160–62
  Cakes, Little French, 187–88
  Cookie Crust, 177
  Mint Sticks, 189–90

195

198

199